P9-EER-447

METHOD SONGWRITING

METHOD SONGWRITING

The Method Used by Professionals

BUDDY KAYE

ST. MARTIN'S PRESS
NEW YORK

"The Best of My Love," words and music by Don Henley, Glenn Frey, and John David Souther, © 1974 Cass County Music, Red Cloud Music & WB Music Corp. All rights reserved. Used by permission.

"Calling Cloud Nine," words by Buddy Kaye, © 1988 Budd Music Corp. (ASCAP). All rights reserved. Used by permission.

"A Crowded Room," words by Buddy Kaye, © 1988 Budd Music Corp. All rights reserved. Used by permission.

"Cry Me a River," by Arthur Hamilton, © 1953 by Bruce Gaitsch & Chappell & Co., Inc. Copyright renewed. International copyright secured. All rights reserved. Used by permission.

"Didn't We," words and music by Jimmy Webb, © 1967, 1969 Jobete Music Co., Inc. Used by permission. All rights reserved. International copyright secured.

"Faretheewell Felice," words by Buddy Kaye, © 1988 Budd Music Corp. All rights reserved. Used by permission.

"Georgia in a Jug," by Bobby Braddock, © 1977, 1978 Tree Publishing Co.,Inc. All rights reserved. Used by permission.

"The Great Indoors," words and music by Wood Newton and Buddy Kaye, © 1983 Budd Music Corp. All rights reserved. Used by permission.

"Happy Birthday, Dear Heartache," words and music by Mack David and Archie Jordan, © 1982 Collins Court Music, Inc. International copyright secured. All rights reserved. Used by permission.

"I Don't Remember Loving You," by Bobby Braddock and Harlan Howard, © 1981 Tree Publishing Co., Inc. All rights reserved. Used by permission.

Acknowledgments continue on page 184.

Design by Glen M. Edelstein

Library of Congress Cataloging-in-Publication Data

Kaye, Buddy.
Method songwriting / by Buddy Kaye.
p. cm.
ISBN 0-312-01790-1
1. Lyric writing (Popular music) I. Title.
MT67.K39 1988
784.5'0028—dc19 87-38271

First Edition

10 9 8 7 6 5 4 3 2 1

Lovingly dedicated to
Matthew and Savanna,
whose tiny veins carry
the seeds of songs unsung.

It is not necessary that you be wealthy or famous or a genius in order to fulfill your own destiny. All that is asked is that you use whatever gifts you have to the best of your ability. If your skill is with a hammer, build! If you have a knack with a hoe, plant! If you are happy on the water, fish! If a pen does your bidding, write! God has never created a nobody.

—Og Mandino and Buddy Kaye
The Gift of Acabar

CONTENTS

TWENTY SONGWRITING TECHNIQUES

ADDENDA

PREFACE

For the past hundred years, as the popular song form has taken shape, the progress of the new songwriter learning to master the craft of writing songs has been slow and agonizing. Relying on intuition and inspiration alone has its share of insurmountable drawbacks, as I personally discovered in the early days of my own career.

The fact is, after the first outpouring of lyrical and melodic inspiration, a song should be built with precision and quality. And just as there are blueprints for the construction of automobile motors, bridges, and skyscrapers, I realized that the song, which is based on *construction* of another kind, demanded a "blueprint" of its own.

Having experienced and overcome years of discouragement, rejection, and inconsistency of product as a young writer, I seized the opportunity, as a seasoned pro, to teach songwriting at UCLA Extension in order to expand a personal system of writing that had produced amazing results for me. Feedback from students and thousands of questions and answers became the basis for communicating a craft that was considered impossible to teach effectively. The perfection of the "blueprint" was in progress.

Method Songwriting is the first work to set forth all the strategies and fundamental components of songwriting—the intricate parts and pieces contained in every successful song written in the past and being written today. It is the world's first detailed step-by-step plan for writing commercial songs. The system is easy to understand and easy to learn.

The selected information in this all-encompassing course in songwriting will feed you professional insights, "tricks of the trade," hard facts, and shortcuts—everything you need to know to help you attain your ultimate potential as a songwriter. As they have done for thousands of songwriters, the Techniques and SongTopics of *Method Songwriting* are designed to trigger your "song-awareness," suggest new working habits, develop productivity, and nourish your imagination.

In songwriting, you could ignore all the fundamentals and simply trust your luck. But if you are looking for a simple, workable, time-saving system for writing commercial songs—one that can awaken and develop your own natural talent—this book is for you.

Welcome to *The Method!* It works!

—BUDDY KAYE
Los Angeles, California

STUDY GUIDELINES

Method Songwriting is the total guide to professional songwriting. The success and implementation of this *step-by-step* method depends on diligence and perseverance.

RULES OF LEARNING:

- The skill-building techniques and topics should be *studied* slowly and thoughtfully—not merely read.

- Each technique should be put into repeated practice before you proceed to the next one. Whether you are a beginning writer or an old hand with a pen, you will gain the most from *Method Songwriting* if you underline and memorize critical information so that it is easily accessible during the creative process.

- Mastering each technique will enable you to analyze quickly the positive and negative elements of *every* song you hear, including your own.

- The final step is to reach into yourself, apply the *step-by-step* knowledge you have acquired, and write your songs for the commercial markets or for your own enjoyment.

TWENTY SONGWRITING TECHNIQUES

TECHNIQUE #1

Starting with a Title

The Seed of Songwriting

The root of a song is in its title. The title is the lyrical "seed" that songwriters cultivate into a "word-bouquet" of sentiment, emotion, and inspiration.

Fresh, original titles *inspire*. Trite titles often lead you, the writer, into trite lines.

An interesting, compelling title has the magnetic power to capture a listener's attention quickly: It's the first thing he or she hears! If your title is unique—different—the listener will be drawn to it. A title can have a certain excitement: It will evoke the storyline; it will push you along and give you the foundation and incentive to complete your song.

Uncommon titles with original storylines have become so valuable that Hollywood producers pay large sums of money for the right to expand them into feature films. Just a few recent examples have been:

La Bamba
Girls Just Want to Have Fun
The Gambler
Ode to Billy Joe
Harper Valley PTA
Take This Job and Shove It!

The song title can be short and direct as in *I Will Survive*. It can be a long title, as in Paul Simon's *One Man's Ceiling*

Is Another Man's Floor. It can also be a short title with a subtitle, as in the country song *She Got the Gold Mine (I Got the Shaft)*. Many published writers, who are not fully aware of the importance of song titles, will make the mistake of choosing a line or an isolated phrase from *somewhere* in the lyric as the title of their song. This lack of professional knowledge can prove costly in the long run. A title that is not unique enough to be memorable can easily be forgotten and never again recorded by other artists at other times.

The process of titling a song should not be considered the same as the process used in finding a name for a novel, a motion picture, or a play. Since a song title requires repetition throughout the lyric, it must be unique and memorable.

It takes only one *uncommon* word to make a title memorable. An uncommon word is a word that may not be unusual in itself, but rather one rarely found in song titles. The word "decorated" is not particularly unique, but when joined with other words not normally associated with it, as in the song *You Decorated My Life,* it becomes a distinctly out-of-the-ordinary title and therefore an outstanding one.

Other examples of uncommon words in song titles, in quotation marks, are:

Take It to the "Limit"
The "Union" of the Snake
"Purple" Rain
Young "Turks"
"Freeze Frame"
When "Doves" Cry
Total "Eclipse" of the Heart
Like a "Virgin"
"Flame Thrower"
"Power Play"
"Centerfold"

An exceptional title usually contains words that are rooted in everyday conversation, but heightened by the art of combining them innovatively.

"Standout" examples:

Old Flames Can't Hold a Candle to You
Good Time Charlie's Got the Blues
Lucy in the Sky with Diamonds
She Blinded Me with Science
Don't Rain on My Parade

Writers of country songs, especially, look for distinctive titles to create instant curiosity:

Whoever Turned Her On Forgot to Turn Her Off
War Is Hell (On the Home Front Too)
Living Here, Loving There and Lying in Between

WHERE DO YOU FIND TITLES?

- In everyday conversation
- Eavesdropping where people gather
- In motion picture dialogue
- In soap operas and talk shows
- In poetry, newspapers and magazines
- In racing forms

HOW DO YOU FIND TITLES?

- By doing lots of reading and scanning for phrases.
- Overall, by keeping your listening "antennae" high,

and by being able to recognize a catchy phrase whenever and wherever you may hear it.

HOW DO YOU KNOW WHEN YOU HAVE A GOOD TITLE?

Have a dialogue with yourself. Ask yourself:

- Is it different from other titles and topics?
- Will the title inspire me?
- Can I comfortably handle the subject matter?
- Will the title give me something important to say?
- Will the record buyer relate to it?

Your answers to these questions will tell you whether the title is worthy of your time, serious thought, and a place in your inventory ledger of song titles for future completion.

PRO INFO:

- Program yourself to mentally catch unusual written and verbal dialogue.
- When you find an original title, jot it down immediately and transfer it later to your stockpile of titles.
- Titles are the songwriter's inventory. Add to your inventory daily.
- A title is like clay—mold it into an idea. For example: The standard song *I Was Lucky* is only a title. Add "to Be Born at the Same Time as You" and you have an idea.
- A good title suggests mood, style, atmosphere, tempo, and direction.

Working alone or with a collaborator, there is no easier way to begin a song than by starting with a title.

THE PROCESS OF FINDING A TITLE IN CONVERSATION

SCENARIO

INSTRUCTOR (*pointing to a student*): You and I are going to create a good song title in the next thirty seconds. Do you believe it can be done?

STUDENT: I don't know. Maybe.

INSTRUCTOR: You realize that the best song titles come from ordinary conversation.

STUDENT: I guess so.

INSTRUCTOR: So . . . if a good title can come out of ordinary conversation, and all of us are constantly yakking, then we have to believe that we speak in titles. Yes?

STUDENT: It sounds reasonable.

INSTRUCTOR: If this is so, you should have hundreds of titles. I'm sure you have lots of conversations. Do you have lots of titles?

STUDENT: No, I don't.

INSTRUCTOR: Would you venture a guess as to why you don't?

STUDENT: I guess I never thought about it.

INSTRUCTOR: But you've just done it!

STUDENT: What did I do?

INSTRUCTOR: You spoke a title.

STUDENT: I did? What did I say?

INSTRUCTOR: *I Never Thought About It.*

STRATEGY

Following is the continuing process of expanding your title into a lyric:

1. If the phrase *I Never Thought About It* appeals to your song sense, it can be a more usable title when you connect it to a subtitle (And Then It Was Too Late). The whole title is now *I Never Thought About It (And Then It Was Too Late).*
2. We have now taken a title and turned it into an idea.
3. Using the same title and a different subtitle for a country ballad, the story may well be *I Never Thought About It (And Now There's Nothing Else I Think About)*

Can you think of another personal situation where the title *I Never Thought About It* can be developed into a commercial ballad? Attempt to find your own idea, your own combination of words.

The accumulation of your inventory of titles begins with the assignment below. Each of the five categories represents the large variety of titles used by professional songwriters in their quest for writing hit songs. (It is often said that there are no *new* story plots. But the creative songwriter finds a way of expressing the old ones in a distinctive way.

ASSIGNMENT: COLLECTING TITLES

In addition to listening and scanning for titles, create a five-category list of your own:

1. A one-word title such as these famous songs:
Faith
Physical
Anticipation
Reunited
Fame

2. A title using contrary or opposite words:
Ebony and Ivory
Your Good Girl's Gonna Go Bad
Peanuts and Diamonds
Midnight Girl in a Sunset Town

3. A cliché, a familiar phrase written cleverly:
I Heard It Through the Grapevine
When You're Hot, You're Hot
Nine to Five

4. A play on words:
Dancing in the Sheets

A Million Light Beers Ago
I Had Too Much to Dream Last Night
Now I Lay Me Down to Cheat

5. An amusing or offbeat song:
Splish Splash
Short People
Winchester Cathedral
Speedy Gonzales
Yellow Submarine

TECHNIQUE #2

Working from a Synopsis

Establishing Your Story

Once the title, style (rock, pop, country, etc.), and specific idea of the song are firmly fixed in your mind, you are ready to outline the complete storyline from your title. This *synopsis* or summary, written in a natural manner of speaking, will become your "blueprint" and will enable you to detail your plot from start to finish.

This method, both simple and practical, further helps you to clarify and organize your thinking in terms of a logical storyline. For example, if you cannot find a satisfying ending in your synopsis, you certainly will not find one in your lyrical refinement. Starting without this detailed plan of information often results in an incomplete song. The time spent on incomplete lyrics can better be spent on other, more complete, ideas that you may have in your inventory of titles.

Forming your synopsis is accomplished by thinking of what you want to say, visualizing the situation in your mind's eye, and transferring your ideas to your worksheet.

If your song idea stems from your own experience, crystallize your reactions, your emotions. If the experience is imaginary or based on another person's experience, recreate those thoughts and reactions with the same realism as if these things had happened to you. Later, you will go into your lyrical self to find the precise words to describe them emotionally.

In essence, the first rule for completing more songs is to outline your entire story in the form of a synopsis *before* beginning your lyric. By following this method, you will have given yourself a detailed "road map" of where you are going, and the most desirable road to travel to finish your song.

PRO INFO:

- There are limitless approaches and story variations in each song title waiting for an imaginative storyteller.
- In your wanderings, collect beginnings for songs—opening lines, provocative thoughts, and situations.
- As the final synopsis for your storyline, choose the one with which you are most comfortable—the subject you can handle, the idea you have experienced or would like to experience.

ASSIGNMENT

1) Review the list of titles that you have prepared for your first assignment.
2) Choose one title as the basis of a synopsis.
3) Think of several approaches for that one title.
4) Choose the approach that has the greatest appeal to you. This will be the storyline that you will eventually develop into a song lyric.

NOTE: If you find that you cannot create a synopsis to your satisfaction, the information in the next step, *Technique #3,* will be helpful.

TECHNIQUE #3

The Three-Minute Movie

The Beginning, Middle, and End

A song is called a three-minute movie because *three minutes is the average time of a single recording*. (Three minutes is also the average time of a rock video.)

As songwriters we must rethink the writing of songs because of the way music is presented and promoted today. Cable and television rock videos are produced to expose and sell the image of today's rock groups and their new music.

The cable outlet MTV became the first video messenger to introduce fans to music presented as mini-musicals. Visual productions, based on lyrical content, dramatically present a deeper dimension of the song with which record companies hope to create LP sales.

However, let's begin by considering *full-length* movies—those that run approximately two hours on the screen.

All good motion pictures have several things in common: *fascinating characters, absorbing plots, sharp dialogue, common conflicts, changes of scene, valid resolutions,* and *surprise endings*—all in all, logically developed stories that continue to move forward and intrigue the audience from start to finish.

This combination of elements is precisely what a good song should have. And, like a movie, a good song should have an organized, well-thought-out *beginning, middle,* and *end.*

Another way of saying it: *crisis, conflict,* and *climax.*

PRO INFO:

The *beginning* of a song usually presents a problem, a conflict, a situation, or a setting—at times, a combination of several of these elements. (NOTE: The *uninteresting* beginning rarely finds anyone staying around for the ending in a movie, or in a song.)

The *middle* examines how the main character is affected by the problem or how the problem is dealt with.

The *end* is the solution to the conflict or problem. Positive endings are preferred by music publishers and recording artists.

Although all three elements (beginning, middle, and end) are of equal importance for a lyric to have fullness and impact, the *end* of a song has its own characteristics. That is where the meaning rests.

A good ending in a play evokes applause. A high C in an operatic aria does likewise. Song lyrics, too, should reach for an emotional, climactic response through an unpredictable ending.

A crafty lyricist continues to lure his listeners with a sense of excitement, and then ends the song with:

- The unexpected twist
- The play on words
- The surprise ending

The "unexpected twist" came in Harry Chapin's song *Taxi*. We learn, in the last section of the song, exactly how his lady friend became an "actress" of sorts, and how Harry became a "flyer" without an airplane. *Taxi* provides an effective role model for students who are interested in writing story songs.

The "play on words" technique was the nucleus for a hit song titled *Thoughtless:*

And maybe if I thought less of you, baby
You wouldn't be so *thoughtless* of me.

The "surprise ending" was used dramatically in Bobbie Gentry's *Ode to Billy Joe*. The mystery question that haunted the listeners was: "What was thrown off the Tallahatchie Bridge?"

It becomes obvious that planning ahead for a unique lyrical ending can add commercial value to your song. Planning the ending of your lyric should be part of the process of formulating the synopsis of your lyrical storyline.

Visualizing a song as a mini-movie is helpful in crafting and controlling the overall perspective of your work.

A song with plot and imagery will suggest to the video producer the sharp focus you envision for the action and elements of your lyrical story when it qualifies for a TV video production.

ASSIGNMENT

Using the information learned from this technique, choose a song title from your inventory and prepare a storyline lyric, in synopsis form, that contains a beginning, middle, and ending that you believe would gain the attention of your listeners.

TECHNIQUE #4

Associated Words

Aid for Accelerated Writing

Associated words are words in the lyric of your song that directly relate to an important key word in the title.

This simple, preparatory technique is designed to enrich your lyrics. A list of associated words will supply you with a storehouse of ideas to inspire you and smoothly facilitate your writing.

In the song *You're Getting to Be a Habit with Me,* featured in the hit Broadway show *42nd Street,* the key word in the title is *habit.*

Words and phrases that are related to, or are associated with, the word *habit* are italicized in the following lyric:

YOU'RE GETTING TO BE A HABIT WITH ME

Words by Al Dubin
Music by Harry Warren

Every kiss, every hug
Seems to act just like a *drug*
You're getting to be a habit with me

Let me stay in your arms
I'm *addicted* to your charms
You're getting to be a habit with me

I used to think your love was something that I
Could *take or leave* alone
But now I couldn't do without *my supply*
I *need* you for my own

Oh, I *can't break away,* I *must have you every day,*
As *regularly as coffee or tea*
You've got me in your *clutches* and *I can't get free*
You're getting to be a *habit* with me *(can't break it!)*
You're getting to be a *habit* with me.

Clearly observe how each of the associated words and phrases helps to reinforce the key word *habit.*

The skillful use of these related words contributes immeasurably to the smoothness and style of the lyric.

The ultimate usage of associated words was achieved in the lyrical gem *Windmills of Your Mind,* in which every line of imagery describes revolving round objects, cylinders, and spheres: the motion of the windmill. This masterpiece, with lyrics by Marilyn and Alan Bergman, and music by Michel Legrand, should be studied in its entirety. Following are the opening lyric lines for those who may have forgotten how very special this song is:

Round like a circle in a spiral
Like a wheel within a wheel
Never ending or beginning
On an ever spinning reel

Opportunities to use associated words do not appear in all song lyrics. Many love songs, including *Just the Way You Are, Feelings,* and *We've Only Just Begun,* rely on warm, sincere, simply stated expressions to evoke emotions of the listeners.

▌PRO INFO: ▌

- When you have a title that has a key word, jot down your list of associated words *before* you actually start writing.
- Place these words in a column on the left-hand margin of your writing page. This will keep them conveniently close as a reference.

Following is another example of a standard song that made excellent use of associated words. The key word is *teach.*

TEACH ME TONITE

Lyric by Sammy Cahn
Music by Gene DePaul

Did you say I've got a lot to learn?
Well, don't think I'm trying not to learn
Since this is the perfect spot to learn
Teach me tonite.

Starting with the "A, B, C" of it,
Right down to the "X, Y, Z" of it,
Help me solve the mystery of it,
Teach me tonite.

The sky's a blackboard high above you
If a shooting star goes by,
I'll use that star to write I love you
A thousand times across the sky.

One thing isn't very clear, my love,
Should the teacher stand so near, my love,
Graduation's almost here, my love,
Teach me tonite.

ASSIGNMENT: RECOGNIZING ASSOCIATED WORDS

List the words and phrases that are associated with the key word *teach:*

______ ______ ______

______ ______ ______

______ ______ ______

ASSIGNMENT: SELECTING ASSOCIATED WORDS

1. Create a list of words and phrases associated with a key word in one of your own titles.
2. Add new associated words to *gamble,* as in

Love Is a Gamble

win	
lose	
lucky	
bet	
taking a chance	
queen of hearts	
calling your bluff	

hot hand __________

cheating at the game __________

Continue with your own list of associated words for the following italicized key words:

There's More Than One Clown at the *Circus*
Heading out to *Hollywood*
Sunday in the *Park*
Country Girl, *City* Boy

TECHNIQUE #5

Form

The Mathematics of Song

With your *title* and *theme* firmly established, your *storyline* and *synopsis* set, and your *associated words* listed in the left-hand column of your working page, you are ready to think about structure. In songwriting, this is called *form*.

The understanding of song form and its effective use is the essence of skillful songwriting.

There are two conventional approaches in deciding what form to use for your song. Some professional writers let the form of their song stem from initial lines they create. Others decide on the form *before* they begin writing.

There are many variations of form in today's popular songs. We will concern ourselves with the three most popular structures which are used in almost all the hit songs you hear on TV, cable, radio, and on records.

A–B–A–B

The most commonly used form in current hit songs is the A–B–A–B structure (verse, "hook" chorus, second verse, repeated "hook" chorus). It is safe to say that 90 percent of the top chart songs are written in this form, including variations.

Sometimes a third section introducing a new music theme is added to the A–B–A–B form. This becomes the "C" section, and this "C" section is called the "bridge." The complete structure or form then becomes A–B–A–B–C–B. Although a "C" section has been added, the form is still referred to as A–B–A–B, with a "bridge."

It is important to note that both A–B–A–B and A–B–A–B–C–B songs always end with the "B" section, the "hook" chorus, which is repeated as the song fades out in a recording.

I was privileged, with my collaborator David Pomeranz, to write a very important gold-record hit for Barry Manilow. The form we chose, one that would most complement our song, was A–B–A–B.

The Old Songs appeared on the *Billboard* hit charts two weeks after its initial release. It was considered a "natural" hit because of its originality in dealing with a subject in songwriting that hadn't been presented.

Like all commercially successful songs, *The Old Songs* should be examined and studied thoughtfully.

THE OLD SONGS

Words and Music by David Pomeranz and Buddy Kaye

Verse 1:

Candles burnin', glasses are chilled
And soon she'll be by.
Hope and pray she'll say that she's
  willing to
Give us another try.
And if all these plans I made
Don't melt the lady's heart,
I'll put on the old forty-fives (and)

"Hook" Chorus:

Maybe the old songs will bring back the
  old times.

Maybe the old lines will sound new.
Maybe she'll lay her head on my
  shoulder.
Maybe old feelings will come through.
Maybe we'll start to cry and wonder why
We ever walked away.
Maybe the old songs will bring back the
  old times
And make her wanna stay.

Verse 2:

It's been too long without seeing her face
Light up when I come home.
It's been too many hours I've wasted
Staring at the phone.
Sweet old songs, I'm counting on you to
Bring her back to me.
I'm tired of list'nin' alone (and)

"Hook" Chorus:

Maybe the old songs will bring back the
  old times.
Maybe the old lines will sound new.
Maybe she'll lay her head on my
  shoulder.
Maybe old feelings will come through.
Maybe we'll start to cry and wonder why
We ever walked away.
Maybe the old songs will bring back the
  old times
And make her wanna stay.

NOTE: In the following A–B–A–B country lyric, because of its up-tempo music, the first "A" verse reached the "hook" chorus too quickly. Another "A" verse had to be added prior to the chorus of *The Great Indoors*.

After the "hook" chorus, normal form was used—a single "A" verse into the repeated chorus.

THE GREAT INDOORS

Words and Music by
Wood Newton and Buddy Kaye

Verse: The week is finally over
(A) I feel it in my bones
Can't wait to start the weekend
The two of us alone
We both are so excited
About what we've got in store
There's nothing like the great indoors

Additional Now you can light the candles
Verse: (A) And I'll just pour the wine
Get high as a mountain
That we don't have to climb
We'll picnic by the fire
On a blanket on the floor
There's nothing like the great indoors

"Hook" Tonight we're camping in again
Chorus: (B) On our king-size bed
Underneath the plaster sky
Eight feet overhead
And when we start in lovin'
Who can ask for more
There's nothing like the great indoors

Verse: The weather here is perfect
(A) The air is your perfume
We'll have a great vacation
And never leave the room
Cause love is here and waiting
Let's reach out and explore
There's nothing like the great indoors

"Hook" Tonight we're camping in again
Chorus: (B) On our king-size bed

Underneath the plaster sky
Eight feet overhead
And when we start in lovin'
Who can ask for more
There's nothing like the great indoors

THE "HOOK"

The "hook" chorus derives its name from the fact that it is designed to literally hook the listener by capturing his or her undivided attention. Each listener is the self-appointed judge and jury of your song. Prior to the record buyer, the *listener* is the music publisher, recording artist, producer, radio station manager, or disc jockey. The success of your A–B–A–B song clearly rides on its "hook."

The strong "hook" chorus contains an ear-catching title that is often used as the *opening line* of the chorus, while the music is "explosive" in feeling, using the upper range of the melody to express intense, genuine emotion. Some examples are:

You Light Up My Life (Recorded by Debby Boone)
Hello (Recorded by Lionel Richie)
Up Where We Belong (Recorded by Joe Cocker and Jennifer Warnes)
What's Love Got to Do with It (Recorded by Tina Turner)

INFORMATIONAL VERSES

A–B–A–B lyrics (with the "A" section using eight lines or the traditional four lines) give the writer the opportunity to tell the whole story of the song without being cramped for space.

The function of informational verses is to lead into and support your simpler, *less* complicated "hook" chorus, for easier listener recall.

The rule is: *Pack the Verses—Broaden the Chorus.*

The following lyric is an example of conversational information unfolding in the verses, leading into a simplistic one-statement chorus:

I LOVE YOU, HONEY, LET'S GO HOME

Lyric by Buddy Kaye
Music by Archie Jordan

Verse 1: (A)

Bet you wonder why I came on by
Knowing what tomorrow brings—
A long day in court, some words from the judge
Slipping off our wedding rings

In these times, divorces happen
A thousand times a day
But I've done a lot of thinkin'
And I've come a long, long way

Chorus: (B)

I love you, honey—who cares who's right or wrong
Let's go home. . . .
I love you, honey,
Let's go home—where we belong

Verse 2: (A)

Everything we built is still in place
Nothing's really changed aroun'

But if we go through with saying "we're through"
It all will come crashing down.

We've put time into this marriage
It deserves another try
It's our one last chance to save it
Before the last good-bye.

Chorus: (B)
I love you, honey—who cares who's right or wrong
Let's go home. . . .
I love you, honey,
Let's go home—where we belong

NOTE: The informational verses of *I Love You, Honey, Let's Go Home* keep the story moving, while the chorus makes one overall statement. This is optimum writing for the A–B–A–B (Verse–"Hook" Chorus–Verse–"Hook" Chorus) song.

PRO INFO:

The function of the verse in the A–B–A–B form is to describe the details, incidents, and situations that lead into the "hook" chorus.

The "hook" chorus makes a single, clear statement relating to the main topic of the song and should not be crowded with details.

"Hook" chorus lines do not change; they are repeated. Repetition makes a song memorable. Occasionally there are songs in which the lines in the chorus change. These are the exceptions to the rule.

As previously stated, there are many variations of song form. Always feel free to experiment. If you are into a "stream-of-consciousness" style of writing, even free form has its roots in the classical form of popular songs. However, it is advisable to learn the rules before you break them.

ASSIGNMENT

Sample of a "hook" chorus requiring verses:

A CAN'T-MISS SITUATION

It was a can't-miss situation
Love was tender, love was strong
It was a can't-miss situation
What went wrong?

Because of the general nature of the chorus, the details of the verses are open to any direction your imagination will take you. It is early in the course for such an assignment, but it may be fun to try it.

Following is a natural storyline you may consider for the verses to be written in the A–B–A–B form:

A. *Verse 1*—Synopsis: "The instant we met we knew we were right for each other . . . We cared, we shared . . . We enjoyed being together . . . Doing the same things . . . When we touched we found love. Then one night you drew away from me . . . It was as though an old memory of someone else had come back to haunt you."
B. Into "hook" chorus: *A Can't-Miss Situation*
A. *Verse 2*—Synopsis: "What can I do to get us back to where we were? I don't think I can make it without you." . . . and so on.
B. Repeat "hook" chorus: *A Can't-Miss Situation*

NOTE: When you have completed the study of the Twenty Techniques, refer back to this assignment and reconstruct your lyrical lines so that they lead logically into the "hook" chorus of *A Can't-Miss Situation*.

GUIDELINES FOR THE "HOOK" CHORUS

Music publishers say: "Don't bore us. Get to the chorus!"

- In other words, have you come to the chorus as quickly as possible or are your verses lengthy to a point where you have lost the interest of the audience?
- Are the title and "hook" chorus repeated enough times so that they leave a strong impression on the mind of the listener?
- Do you have a chorus that clearly follows the verses and ties the sections together?
- Do your verses contain specific details that lead into and support the chorus?
- Do you need a "bridge" for additional lyrical information prior to your last repeat of the "hook" chorus?

This concludes information on the A–B–A–B form.

A–A–B–A

In the A–A–B–A form, the *first, second* and *fourth* sections (or stanzas) are musically alike in structure. The *third* section is the "B" section, also known as the "bridge" of the song. The "B" section should always have an interesting, innovative change of mood. Lyrically, the length of lines and rhyme scheme of the "B" section should vary from the previous and following "A" sections. After the "B" section, there is always a final "A" section.

Although the music in each "A" section is similar, the words, for the most part, are different.

Keeping in mind this information, analyze the following A–A–B–A song:

OVER THE RAINBOW

Lyric by E. Y. (Yip) Harburg
Music by Harold Arlen

The first "A" section:

Somewhere over the rainbow
Way up high
There's a land that I heard of
Once in a lullaby

The second "A" section:

Somewhere over the rainbow
Skies are blue
And the dreams that you dare to
Dream really do come true

The "B" section or the "bridge" of the song:

Someday I'll wish upon a star
And wake up where the clouds are far behind me
Where troubles melt like lemondrops
Away above the chimney tops,
That's where you'll find me

The final "A" section:

Somewhere over the rainbow
Bluebirds fly
Birds fly over the rainbow
Why then, oh why can't I?

Did you notice the change of mood and rhythmic pace of the lyrics in the "B" section? ("Someday I'll wish upon a star . . ." etc.) The double-time movement was deliberately constructed to add a new dimension to the song and to keep it from becoming monotonous. This is the prime function of the "B" section.

POPULAR STANDARD TITLES AND THE FORMS IN WHICH THEY WERE WRITTEN

A–A–B–A (Stanza, Stanza, Bridge, Stanza)

If (David Gates/Bread)
Yesterday (Beatles)
Saving All My Love for You (Whitney Houston)
New York, New York (Frank Sinatra/Liza Minnelli)
Smoke Gets in Your Eyes (Various artists)
Georgia on My Mind (Ray Charles)
Breaking Up Is Hard to Do (Neil Sedaka)
Help Me Make It Through the Night (Kris Kristofferson)
Just the Way You Are (Billy Joel)

Raindrops Keep Falling on My Head (B. J. Thomas)
Don't It Make My Brown Eyes Blue (Crystal Gayle)

A–B–A–B (Verse, "Hook" Chorus, Verse, "Hook" Chorus)

She Believes in Me (Kenny Rogers)
How Deep Is Your Love (Bee Gees)
You Light Up My Life (Debby Boone)
Three Times a Lady (Lionel Richie/Commodores)
Stand by Me (Ben E. King)
I Write the Songs (Barry Manilow)
One More Night (Phil Collins)
I'll Never Love This Way Again (Dionne Warwick)

A–B–A–C

A third form used occasionally in song construction is known as the A–B–A–C structure.

The A–B–A–C songs contain three distinct, but integrated, musical sections. Among the world's most famous songs using the A–B–A–C form are:

Deep Purple
Moon River
Stardust
Till the End of Time
When I Fall in Love

Following is the lyric of a very popular A–B–A–C song.

SING

Words and Music by Joe Raposo

"A" Sing!
Sing a song.
Sing out loud
Sing out strong.

"B" Sing of good things, not bad,
Sing of happy, not sad.

Altered "A" Sing!
Sing a song.
Make it simple
To last your whole life long.

"C" Don't worry that it's not good enough
For anyone else to hear
Sing!
Sing a song!

The changes in the four stanzas are beautifully coordinated to form a thirty-two-bar song that flows perfectly.

OTHER FORMS (UNCOMMON)

A–A–A–A: *He's Got the Whole World in His Hands*

A–A–B–C: *The Star-Spangled Banner*

A–B–C–D: *God Bless America*

PRO INFO:

The form of a song is rarely questioned by music publishers or recording artists if it sounds and feels natural. As a rule, almost any song form is acceptable as long as the sections, musically and lyrically, flow easily into one another.

In due course, if you wish to establish a form for your song when you have only a lyrical idea and are not sure of your direction, simply start writing your lyric to an *established* melody that is similar in mood to your idea.

When the new lyric is complete, create your own new melody to your original lyric or present the lyric to your collaborator without mentioning the source of your inspiration. Allow your collaborator the freedom of creativity before divulging your secret.

ASSIGNMENT

1. To understand different song forms, analyze your favorite songs (contemporary and standard).
2. Figure out in which forms they were written.
3. Type or print the lyric of one such song. In the left-hand column, in large block letters, write the alphabetical letters to describe the form of the song.

Knowing the "mechanics" of an art allows you to concentrate and plan strategies to develop the product.

—Anonymous

TECHNIQUE #6

Title Repetition and Title Placement

TITLE REPETITION

Repetition is considered a law of learning. The more frequently the title of a song is repeated, the more deeply it will become ingrained in the mind of the listener.

The practical reason for title repetition is to identify your song to the radio listener. Many record producers, striving for hit *sounds,* give low priority to audible clarity of lyrics. Lyrics that are buried in incessant percussion beats and shrieking guitars add a degree of anonymity to a song. In other instances, radio deejays do not announce song titles between recordings of songs. (Radio time is expensive!) Yet your title must be heard to be remembered.

Hit songs, of course, are still possible for those who do not follow the title repetition rule. However, once the hit has come and gone, it becomes extremely difficult to recall the name of the song from among the thousands that flood the airwaves year in and year out. Chances for a "cover record" (an old song revived by a new artist at a later time) are virtually impossible.

Title repetition can also be a powerful tool for enhancing the emotional impact of a song. Example: *You're No Good,* the title-repetitive Linda Ronstadt hit song of some years ago. In the Lennon-McCartney classic, *Yesterday,* the title was used as the *first* and *last* word of every stanza of the A–A–B–A song. In the rhythm-and-blues standard, *Sunny,* the title is used three times in every section of the song.

TITLE PLACEMENT

There is no rule in songwriting as to where a title should appear in a lyric. However, some places in a song are less effective than others.

For example: A title placed in the *middle* of a verse or stanza can sound more like a *line* in the lyric rather than an important title.

There are three strategic places for effective placement of your title. (Review the songs in your mind.)

1. In the *first line* of the "hook" chorus (A–B–A–B form), as in:

Rhinestone Cowboy
I Write the Songs
You Light Up My Life
You've Lost That Loving Feeling

2. In the *first line* of each "A" section (A–A–B–A form), as in:

Blue Moon
Yesterday
Raindrops Keep Falling on My Head

3. In the *last line* of each "A" section (A–A–B–A form), as in:

> *New York, New York*
> *As Time Goes By*
> *Smoke Gets in Your Eyes*
> *Breaking Up Is Hard to Do*
> *Help Me Make It Through the Night*

PRO INFO:

The decision for placement of the title in your lyric should be made when you are establishing the form (*Technique* #4) of your lyric. The form should begin to take place in your mind when you are preparing your synopsis (*Technique* #2).

Think of your song title as a commercial trademark. The more prominent and distinctive it is, the more memorable it will be for record buyers, recording artists and producers of the future.

ASSIGNMENT

1. Learn the technique of effective title placement by researching and analyzing current chart songs and favorite standards.

2. Transcribe to paper the lyrics of two familiar songs in each category:

- **A.** Where the title is used as the *first line* of the A–B–A–B "hook" chorus.
- **B.** Where the title is used as the *first line* of each "A" section of the A–A–B–A form.
- **C.** Where the title is used as the *last line* of each "A" section of the A–A–B–A form.

TECHNIQUE #7

Meter and Syllables

The Rhythm of the Words

Let's begin by giving the definitions of two elements used in the construction of lyrical lines.

Meter: Rhythmic patterns of accented and unaccented notes or beats.

Syllables: A word or part of a word pronounced with a single, uninterrupted sound. The word "love" has one syllable; the word "lovely" has two syllables; the word "lovable" has three syllables.

Once you have established a lyrical pattern of meter and syllables in the first verse (or stanza) of your lyric, the *fixed pattern* of accented and unaccented words becomes a *model* for that section of your song, which will be repeated.

Using *Over the Rainbow* again as an example, take notice of how precisely the meter (the accents) and the number of syllables in each line of the first, second, and fourth stanzas are perfectly matched.

Somewhere over the rainbow	7 syllables
Way up high	3 syllables
There's a land that I heard of	7 syllables
Once in a lullaby	6 syllables
Somewhere over the rainbow	7 syllables
Skies are blue	3 syllables

And the dreams that you dare to — 7 syllables
Dream really do come true — 6 syllables

The final "A" stanza in the A–A–B–A song matches the accents and the number of syllables established in stanzas one and two:

Somewhere over the rainbow — 7 syllables
Bluebirds fly — 3 syllables
Birds fly over the rainbow — 7 syllables
Why, then, oh why can't I? — 6 syllables

ACCENTED WORDS

Counting syllables in lyric lines is not always the correct answer for matching lyrics verse to verse, as the following stanza will reveal.

The moon hangs high in the sky — 7 syllables
And smiles down — 3 syllables
You can see him wink his eye — 7 syllables
From the top of the town — 6 syllables

The four random lines, above, have something in common with the first four lines of *Over the Rainbow*. They have the same number of syllables. Yet the words do not fit the familiar music of *Over the Rainbow*. Why? Because the accent of the words in the "Moon" song is different from the accent of the words in *Over the Rainbow,* although both have the same number of syllables.

The true test is for you to try to sing the "Moon" words to the music of *Over the Rainbow*. This is an important test.

Quality writing calls for smooth-flowing lyrics that do not vary in meter and syllables from verse to verse. To ensure consistency, syllables should be rhythmically reviewed as to where the strong and weak words fall in each repeating verse or stanza.

Free-form lyric lines that ignore exactness of meter and syllables may be easier to create but they present problems. Using more syllables in one verse than another automatically necessitates a change in the music to *accommodate* this unevenness.

PRO INFO:

1. The meter and syllable pattern you establish in Verse #1 must be continued in the verses that follow if the music is the same.
2. For those who write words and music, a simple test is to place the words of Verse #1 under the notes of the music, followed by the placement of the words in Verse #2 under the same notes. This will permit you to see if you have an insufficient number of words, an excess number of words, or if both lyric verses fit perfectly under the musical notes.
3. The rule to follow is: important words fall on accented beats. These important words are usually nouns (the names of things) and verbs (action words). Unimportant words such as "a," "an," and "the" are never used as accented downbeats.
4. Being forced into writing a lyric line of fixed meter and syllables (so that one verse scans with the other) makes you dig more deeply to express your thoughts and ideas. In doing so, there is a strong possibility that you will write more inspired and effective lines.

This is how songs of quality are created.
This is how standard works are born.

ASSIGNMENT: METER

Continue the lyric stanza below, matching the number of syllables in each new line and conforming to the rhyme scheme. Your lines, obviously, should extend the mood of the storyline. Aim your verse toward the "hook" chorus titled

Your Place or Mine

It was a quiet party
Until our eyes caught sight
It only took a moment
To know we'd share the night

____

____

____

____

Once you have completed your part of the newly written stanza, consider writing the "hook" chorus, *Your Place or Mine*.

To complete your song, you should follow your "hook" chorus with another verse that leads back to the repeated "hook" chorus for a final time.

NOTE: Only attempt the above assignment when you feel you are ready to undertake the task.

TECHNIQUE #8

Rhymes

Creating Word Sounds

Rhymes are based on sound, not spelling—for example, "first" is a perfect rhyme for "rehearsed."

Rhymes draw attention to words.

Rhymes make lines easier to remember.

Rhymes add richness to a lyric with sounds that are pleasing to the ear.

People have grown up with rhymes, ranging from the Mother Goose rhymes of our childhood to the latest commercial jingles on radio and television.

CREATIVE RHYMING

Imagination in creative rhyming is important. With imagination, you can invent your own rhymes by combining words.

In Paul Williams's lyric of *You and Me Against the World,* a seemingly impossible word to rhyme, "circus," is rhymed with a combination of *two* words, "overwork us."

In the song *These Foolish Things,* the single word "apartment" is rhymed with two words, "heart meant."

A tinkling piano in the next apartment
Those stumbling words that told me what your heart meant

DOUBLE RHYMING

Double rhyming is accomplished by having two words in one line rhyme with two words in the next line. An example of such creative rhyming is found in the song *Faretheewell Felice,* written for George Benson's particular jazz-rock style. The double rhyming words are italicized in the following excerpt from this song:

No more *wick left*—in the *candle*
No more *kick left*—soon the *band'll*
Play the last song and our love will die,
Fare thee well, Felice—Good-bye!

INNER RHYMES

An *inner rhyme* is a rhyme which occurs in the middle of a lyric line in addition to the normal rhyme at the end of the line. In the standard song *Ten Cents a Dance,* lyricist Lorenz Hart rhymes "hero" with "queer romance." Johnny Mercer was a master of inner rhymes, as in *Tangerine:*

Tangerine—She is all they claim
With her eyes of *night* and lips as *bright* as flame,
Tangerine—When she dances by
Senoritas *stare* and caball*eros* sigh.

IMPERFECT RHYMES

Definition: Two words that *sound* alike, but have word endings where the consonants don't agree.

Imperfect rhymes are also called "soft" rhymes and "false" rhymes.

TRUE RHYMES VS. FALSE RHYMES

It has become fashionable for many contemporary writers to use "false" rhymes (stressing the sound of the vowel rather than the precise consonant), such as rhyming "mi*n*e" with "ti*m*e," . . . "grea*t*" with "ma*k*e"—and sometimes dropping the consonants, as in rhyming "roa*d*" with "go." Although this casual form of rhyming is acceptable today, there is still an unequaled ring of satisfaction at the sound of a *true* rhyme.

When you reach for true rhymes, you are forcing yourself to stretch creatively for more than an easy, automatic solution. The extra effort usually gives your finished product a much finer quality.

If you decide to strive for true rhymes, you should use a rhyming dictionary to verify your rhyming words. Using true rhymes in your lyrics may not guarantee you a hit, and, the record-buying public may not even notice the difference, but the people in the music industry will. Your professional image is reflected in the craftsmanship of every song you write.

The choice between the traditional and the free-form, sound-alike approach to rhyming, is simply the choice you make as a lyricist. However, as a new writer, your lyric priority should be to attain meaningful lines over perfect rhymes. Once you become more experienced, your target should be to achieve both objectives.

The following is an example in excellence of clear thought, innovative rhymes, and the use of *inner* rhymes (in italics):

ONE FOR MY BABY
(And One More for the Road)

Lyric by Johnny Mercer
Music by Harold Arlen

It's quarter to three,
There's no one in the place except you and me,
So, set 'em up Joe,
I've got a little story you oughta know,
We're drinking, my *friend,*
To the *end* of a brief episode,
So make it one for my baby
And one more for the road.

I got the routine,
So drop another nickel in the machine,
I'm feelin' so bad,
I wish you'd make the music dreamy and sad,
Could tell you a *lot,*
But you've *got* to be true to your code,
Make it one for my baby
And one more for the road.

You'd never know it,
But Buddy, I'm a kind of poet,
And I've gotta lotta things to say,
And when I'm gloomy,
You simply gotta listen to me,
Until it's talked away.

Well, that's how it goes
And Joe, I know you're getting anxious to close,
So thanks for the cheer,
I hope you didn't mind my bending your ear,
This torch I've *found,*
Must be *drowned* or it soon might explode,

Make it one for my baby
And one more for the road.
That long, long road.

PRO INFO:

- Rhymes are a critical component to the acceptability of a lyric: They enrich the sound, they attract attention, and, most importantly, they aid the listener in remembering the words.
- A new writer should not be overly concerned with the "true" or "false" rhyme—the effective thought or idea should be paramount in this decision. As the writer improves, the perfection of the "true" rhyme will become a natural desire.
- Repetition of the same rhyming sound (you, blue, do, knew, few, clue, etc.) tends to be monotonous, even though the rhymes appear in different sections of the song. The rule is: once used, a rhyme should not be used again in another section of your lyric.
- Never settle for a superficial line because it leads you to the rhyme. Instead, work the most powerful thought you can think of into one of *many* rhymes that are available. The rule is: always use the rhyme that will provide the strongest line of thought and reason.
- Professionals use: *The Complete Rhyming Dictionary* by Clement Wood (Doubleday), and Sammy Cahn's *The Songwriter's Rhyming Dictionary* (Facts On File Publications).
- Experiment with word combinations: two words that rhyme with a single word. Creative rhyming can be fun.

TECHNIQUE #9

Singable Words

Hard and Soft Syllables

Song lyrics are different from poems. Poems are not usually sung. They are read silently or recited aloud *without* regard to tempo. Singable words and phrases are not an important consideration in writing poetry.

Song lyrics are words joined to other words to form phrases. The professional songwriter combines *hard* and *soft* syllables so that such lyrical phrases are easy to sing. "Strength strikes back" or "First loves die hard" are unsingable phrases because the key words consist of hard sounds (consonants). Too many "s" sounds produce hissing sounds. In contrast, the phrase "without a word of warning" is very singable.

The English language contains two dominant sounds:

1. *consonant sounds*—made by blocking the flow of air, as in the harsh word "next."
2. *vowel sounds*—made by allowing the air to flow freely, utilizing the sounds of "a," "e," "i," "o," and "u."

Carefully alternating or mixing consonants and vowels (hard and soft sounds) automatically produces singable lyrics.

Words such as "next" and "that" cannot be comfortably sung at the end of the lyric line. The hard "t" ending for "next" and "that" cuts the sound off abruptly.

For example, if *Mary Had a Little Lamb* were rewritten and the last word was "back," it would be difficult to *sustain* the last note of the refrain. Try it!

Mary lost her little lamb,
He's never coming back.

You probably sounded like Mary's little lamb if you tried to prolong the last word, "b-a-a-ck."

When it is absolutely necessary to use an unsingable word as the last word in your lyric line, the music must compensate by not demanding that the harsh word be sustained vocally. The vocalist should pronounce the word quickly, as in "so that's that," and let the accompanying music continue to the end of the musical phrase.

PRO INFO:

1. Unsingable words present problems! As a lyricist, you are obliged to test the easy flow of your lyrics and correct them, if possible. This is accomplished in the following manner:

A. Sing your lyrics aloud at a comfortable tempo.
B. If you stumble over a word or phrase, seek substitute words that flow vocally or change your rhyme scheme to solve the problem.
C. An excellent test is to sing or speak your lyrics at an accelerated pace (speed them up). You'll find your "moment of truth."

2. Realize that your lyrical lines must ride "piggy-back" on the unyielding tempo of the melody.
3. As a writer, it is your responsibility to eliminate clumsy words or phrases before a recording artist trips over your lyrics, becomes disheartened with your song, and eliminates it in the middle of the recording session.

TECHNIQUE #10

Specifics

Who, When, Where, What, Why, How

The function of *specifics* is to bring essentials to a story, so the listener can bring his own perceptions to that scene, making it personal and familiar to him.

Specifics in songwriting should be unfolded gradually so that the listener, as the song progresses, learns more and more about the subject and the character(s) in the story as it unravels. Details, subtle or bold, make the storyline clearer and help maintain continued interest in the song.

However, there is the song lyric that attains great popularity by virtually eliminating details. Such a lyric makes a *single statement*. The one-statement approach was used successfully in *Don't It Make My Brown Eyes Blue*. The lyrical theme never went beyond the self-pity of the singer, Crystal Gayle, being rejected by the person she loved. The simplified portrayal of hurt feelings and ear-arresting music propelled the song into a universal hit.

More intricate lyrics such as *The Gambler,* introduced by Kenny Rogers, and Paul Simon's *The Boxer* require a potpourri of detail to clarify the various characters and situations. Both hit songs, professionally admired, were written with broad strokes of imagination and are considered to be standard works.

Following are the elements of information found in specifics:

Who—refers to the person who is lyrically relating his or her story, message, or personal feelings. The identity must be crystal clear to the listener as to *who* the person is and what role he or she is portraying in the theme of your Three-Minute Movie (see *Technique #3*). "Who" can be the "grieving lover" by singing *Take Me Back;* a "friend" cautioning, *Don't Mess with Her Man;* or a "narrator" telling the story of *The Gambler*.

Rapid identification of your main character helps the listener relate to subsequent statements the lyric is making. For example, note the instant identification of the character in the first line of Jim Webb's *Wichita Lineman*. The singer tells us he is a lineman who works for the county. The listener can instantly "see" this person and describe the lineman's appearance, his approximate age, his clothes, and so forth. With identification established, the listener can quickly connect with the details of the story as it unravels.

▌PRO INFO: ▌

Recording artists usually choose songs in which the *who* is someone with whom they and their audience can identify.

When—refers to the time frame in which the story is taking place. Is it *Sweet Summer Loving-Time* or *April in Paris?*

The specifics of *when* should be woven into the fabric of your lyric, sometimes subtly, sometimes boldly, but the time element, provided this information is germane to your story, should be clearly defined. Starting your lyric in the frame of "tonight" or "this morning" is a popular way of establishing time.

The detail of *when* can be the title of your song, as in Gordon Lightfoot's *Early Morning Rain,* or can be built into the body of your lyric, as in John Denver's *Leaving on a Jet Plane,* in which the time of departure is specified as early morning.

Where—refers to the place or location of an action—a room, a garden, a train, and so on. A place can be established without actually naming it. For example, in the line "I sit around and wait for your call," the listener's perception leads him or her to understand that the phone call is being received *at home*. If the call were received in a phone booth, it would have been stated.

What—refers to the action of the situation. In the song *Rhinestone Cowboy,* writer Larry Weiss establishes *what* and *where* simultaneously by stating: "I've been walking these streets so long—singing the same old song; I know every crack in these dirty sidewalks of Broadway." His lines clearly tell us *what* he is doing and *where* he is.

Why—refers to the reason for what is taking place. For example: *Why* is the "Rhinestone Cowboy" walking the streets? We soon find out that he is broke and just starting out, but not without "star-spangled" dreams of a rodeo career.

Another *why* that appears in many love songs is *why* someone is leaving somebody else. *Why* has someone fallen in or out of love? Your audience is looking to you for answers.

How—refers to *how* events and situations will be resolved. In a good lyric, if there is conflict, there must be resolution; if there is a problem, there must be an answer or the suggestion of one.

PRO INFO:

The specifics of *who, when, what, why, where,* and *how* are an integral part of *Technique #2—Working from a Synopsis,* and *Technique #3—The Three-Minute Movie.*

The listener knows nothing about the story until the specifics are stated quickly, clearly, and interestingly.

Remember, it is not necessary to utilize *who, when, what, why, where,* and *how* in every set of lyrics that you write. Only use the elements that make the details of your message clear and concise.

The great pleasure in life is doing what people say you cannot do.

—Walter Bagehot

TECHNIQUE #11

Imagery

The Painted Word

Splashing color on dull phrases is the true function of *imagery*. The dictionary defines *imagery* as "figures of speech in beautiful or vivid pictures."

Imagery and specifics can be interrelated. In their classic work for writers and journalists, *The Elements of Style,* William Strunk, Jr., and E. B. White address the topics of imagery and specifics in the following example:

> He showed satisfaction as he took possession of his well-earned reward.

They replace this sentence with the more colorful statement:

> He grinned as he pocketed the coin.

Imagery inspires, motivates, and illustrates, as in this picturesque phrase:

> When you come to a stone wall, paint a door on it . . . and walk through.

PRO INFO:

Imagery, interrelated with specifics, plays an even greater role in lyrics because of the brief time and space allotted to the development of the storyline of a song.

Word pictures in lyrics play a multi-dimensional role. They allow listeners, in their mind's eye, to "see" the action taking place, "smell it," "touch it." It gives them something extra to feel the sensual or emotional impact.

In a dramatic scene in which a woman relates the story of learning that her lover was unfaithful, she has the choice of a stereotypical remark, such as "My world has come to an end," or a line of rage such as "I felt like lightning in a bottle, ready to explode."

The latter, of course, vividly expresses the emotion of jealousy and adds a dynamic quality to the personal statement.

THE IMAGERY PROCESS

The process of adding imagery to your lyric lines, getting into the heart of what you want to describe, can be achieved as follows: Close your eyes, visualize the situation and/or setting you wish to express, get it in clear, sharp focus, and "snap" the picture in colorful language. It is a matter of concentration and practice.

Stretching your imagination can change the most ordinary idea into the picture that paints a thousand words.

PRO INFO:

In today's world of visual marketing of music and self-contained groups, colorful, vivid, imaginative lyric lines have become the significant inspiration to the production of TV and cable rock videos used in promoting new songs to the top of the charts.

ASSIGNMENT: IMAGERY

In as many words as you require, stretch your imagination to creatively complete the following assignment, *avoiding clichés.*

Quiet as ____________________________________

Loud as ____________________________________

Loving as ____________________________________

Angry as ____________________________________

Round as ____________________________________

Swift as ____________________________________

Friendly as ____________________________________

Explosive as ____________________________________

Poor as ____________________________________

Rich as ____________________________________

Brave as ____________________________________

Beautiful as ____________________________________

Hopefully, your descriptive list will, in time, join such evergreens as:

Sly as a fox
Straight as an arrow
Quiet as a mouse
Sharp as a tack
High as a kite
Close as pages in a book

TECHNIQUE #12

Alliteration

Enhancing Word Sounds

Alliteration, often considered an art form in itself, is defined as the repetition of the same letter or sound at the beginning of two or more words, which are adjacent to each other.

It may sound complicated but it's simple. For example, notice the alliteration in the common phrase:

*M*ethod to his *m*adness

In the Rodgers and Hart classic:

Bewitched, Bothered and Bewildered

In the Elvis Presley hit:

Heartbreak Hotel

In the Mel Tillis country hit:

Coca-Cola Cowboy

While some of these phrases may have been coincidental or accidental, it is not uncommon for professional songwriters to seek the smooth-sounding benefits of alliteration in their lyrics.

One of the most delightful examples is found in a song that was written for Judy Garland and her lovable friends in *The Wizard of Oz:*

WE'RE OFF TO SEE THE WIZARD

Lyric by E. Y. (Yip) Harburg
Music by Harold Arlen

We're off to see the Wizard
The wonderful Wizard of Oz
We hear he is, a wiz of a wiz
If ever a wiz there was

If ever a wonderful wiz there was
The Wizard of Oz is one becuz
Becuz, becuz, becuz, becuz, becuzzzzzzzz
Becuz of the wonderful things he does

Alliteration adds a distinctive tonal quality to a lyric and can create an artistic challenge for you as well.

This technique of using alliteration is achieved by researching your key word in *Roget's Thesaurus* and finding substitutes that help you achieve your artistic objectives.

Word substitutions (synonyms) lead to the discovery of nuances and subtle shades of meanings. The abundant range of options that opens for the ambitious writer can eliminate stretches of dull phrases in the story being related.

For example, the writers of a standard ASCAP work were constructing their song using the banal title: "Trust me, darling, because it's true." Instead of this uninspired group of words, the line became: *Believe It, Beloved, Because It's True.*

PRO INFO:

There must always be something in your words and music that is *now* and *new*.

When constructing your lyric, search for words that can achieve alliteration.

Though not absolutely essential, alliteration adds decoration to your song lyric and its value is recognized in the eyes of your professional peers.

ASSIGNMENT: ALLITERATION

Using letters of the alphabet, create original song titles that contain alliteration.

Hit Song Examples:

"L"— Love Me to the Limit

"G"— Your Good Girl's Gonna Go Bad

"P"— Pistol-Packing Mama

"H"— Holding Out for a Hero

"B"— ____________________

"F"— ____________________

"M"— ____________________

"R"— ____________________

TECHNIQUE #13

Language Tone

Regional Colloquialisms

Songs are written in a variety of categories. Among the most popular are: rock, country, middle-of-the-road (pop ballads), gospel, and soul. Each style/category of songs has its own family of variations.

Rock music variations include heavy metal, techno-pop, and reggae.
Country music variations consist of pop/crossover, country rock, soft rock, bluegrass, novelty, ballads, and blues.
Middle-of-the-road songs are geared toward adult-contemporary listeners. Artists in this category include Barry Manilow, Neil Diamond, Melissa Manchester, Carly Simon, Billy Joel, and Paul Simon.
Gospel, religion-inspired music, covers traditional folk and church choral selections which include Judy Collins singing *Amazing Grace* and Elvis Presley singing *How Great Thou Art*. Gospel crossover is referred to as Christian rock-and-roll.
Soul music covers stylized ballads (such as Sam Cooke's *You Send Me* and Ray Charles's *I Can't Stop Loving You*), funk, rhythm and blues. Soul music is occasionally combined with jazz and gospel music.

Each style of music has its own "tone" of lyrics. Regional lyrics can be as varied as an Alabama trucker singing

Convoy or Professor Higgins, in the musical *My Fair Lady,* singing *The Rain in Spain (Falls Mainly on the Plain).*

Language tone is characteristic of lyrics reflecting regional accents and expressions. It is therefore necessary to write in the precise manner that people speak. A problem arises when writers write the way they *think* people speak. Regional hit songs should be analyzed.

Distinction of language tone is the direct result of the way words are combined, the colloquial metaphors, and the rhythm and style of music that expresses the words.

SINGERS AND LYRICS

A lyric is to a singer what dialogue is to an actor or actress. His or her personality is established in the first few words that are spoken or sung. Words that are inconsistent with the song character's personality will give the lyric a false ring and seem artificial. It can distract the listener and totally break the *mood* of a song if just one word is out of character.

PRO INFO:

1. To achieve uniformly strong language tone throughout your entire song, replace unsuitable words or phrases without losing your original thought or idea.
2. Remember that your lyric is only as strong as the weakest line in your song.
3. A sudden change in language tone will "jolt" the concentration of a listener. The listener's attention will be temporarily diverted, thereby leaving a vacuum in his or her comprehension of the feeling or message of your song.

4. Lack of expertise as a writer shows up quickly when you begin dealing with music publishers, record producers and recording artists. Inconsistent language tone is professionally unacceptable.
5. Eloquent, erudite words do not belong in the everyday language that is commonly used in writing lyrics. Occasionally, there is an exception. In *Cry Me a River,* the great standard by Arthur Hamilton, the writer ends the "bridge" of his song calling for an inner rhyme, forcing the use of an obscure word, "plebeian."

You . . . told me love was too *plebeian,*
Told me you were through with *me an'* . . .

The song became an instant hit even though it broke the rule of language tone.

TECHNIQUE #14

Emotional Values

The Heart of the Song

Emotion in a song—the expression of one's deepest feelings through words and music—is that special ingredient which gives a song its power.

Emotional words and music reach out from a small radio speaker and evoke listener reaction, creating and eliciting memories and arousing feelings. A single word is capable of recalling an emotion or stimulating a person's senses.

Emotional values cannot be expressed by the fact that it is raining, but in the feeling of being rained upon.

In music, an original sequence of exotic chord progressions can enrich a simple melody so that it becomes an emotionally haunting refrain.

If you play guitar or piano, you can test the power of chord progressions by playing just a one-finger melody version of George Gershwin's classic *The Man I Love* (or any other popular song that has endured). Then, by adding the fullness of the written chords, you can discover the emotional impact which the chordal progression creates. The melody line by itself does not make a hit. Music notes are *undressed* without chords and unfulfilled without meaningful words.

A song can cause its listeners to reflect, as many listeners did when they heard provocative songs of the 1960s, such as *Abraham, Martin, and John* and *Blowin' in the Wind;* or to be moved by a rendition of Irving Berlin's great classic *God Bless America;* or to be inspired to join in the singing of *The Star-Spangled Banner* as the flag goes by.

Emotional lines can also speak *softly,* as in the ballads *Feelings* and *I Honestly Love You,* and in Lionel Richie's plaintive love songs *Hello* and *Truly.*

HOW CAN YOU JUDGE IF YOUR LYRIC HAS EMOTIONAL POWER?

If you set aside your completed work and return to it later to find it still emotionally effective, chances are your audience will respond as well. The same principle applies to the emotional valule of your music.

In your desire to achieve emotional impact, you must constantly review what you have written. Decide whether your lyrics have set an inspiring tone or if they have unintentionally created a depressing mood.

The following lyric is an example of emotional values in action:

SOMEONE YOU ONCE LOVED

Lyric by Buddy Kaye

You'll *run* to her when she *calls* on the phone
You can *feel* her pain when she's *feeling* alone
You *want* to be there *comforting* her
when her *tears* softly fall . . .
You'll do *anything* for *someone you once loved*
You'll do *anything* at all

If *bills* come in and they're *stamped* overdue
You just *pay* them all, ask "what *else* can I do?"
You're *still* the old team *but* the old dreams
have been *left* far behind. . . .
You'll do *anything* for *someone you once loved*
'Cause she's *always* on your mind

Bridge:

I *know* about love like this
And I'll *never* be the same
And *now* after loving her
My life is *humorously* tame . . .
And I *still* fall . . . all over myself
At the *sound* of her name

I *changed* her life . . . from the *woman* she was
She's no *longer* mine . . . but I *care* what she does
For *all* of my life she'll *always* be
my *best* friend, but then. . . .
You'll do *anything* for *someone you once loved*
But *love* her again

PRO QUESTIONS:

- Is your music built on a sequence of emotional chord progressions that you believe can touch the heart of a listener?
- Is your music warm, melodic, moving in mood and style?
- When read aloud, does your lyric stand on its own?
- Have you become so infatuated with your lyric lines that you have substituted *cleverness* for direct emotional contact?
- Have you written a *private* lyric (naming places and revealing incidents meaningful to you and your

friends), rather than a lyric which has universal appeal?

- Have you thought of your lyric as dialogue for a singer? Is it interesting? Different? Would the singer enjoy the "role" you have created for him or her?

Empathy is the imaginative projection of one's personality into another person. Empathy is the secret of writing. You stop being YOU and become the person.

—ROCKWELL

TECHNIQUE #15

Opening Lines

Words That Command Attention

Songwriters must assume that the majority of record buyers are *passive* listeners. Rather than having their ears "glued" to the radio, stereo, or TV to pick up every emotional nuance in your song, most people actually pay little attention to what they are hearing.

It is only when something unique catches their attention that they respond.

Indifferent, passive listeners can also include record producers, artists, and music publishers if other matters occupy their minds—an uncomfortable position if a writer is demonstrating a song. How do we circumvent this situation?

The opening line—musically and lyrically—is probably the most effective way to get their attention and introduce your song.

SHOCK WORDS

An original beginning, an unusual word, a provocative thought set to an equally seductive melody has a way of announcing itself even to the most passive listener.

The word "Hey!" as in *Hey! Did You Happen to See the Most Beautiful Girl in the World?* or the word "Stop!" as in the Supremes' hit *Stop! In the Name of Love,* act as direct commands to the listener's subconscious mind.

- o Shock words announce the existence of your song.
- o Shock words make people stop and listen.

Provocative statements, as found in the first two lines of the Eagles' hit song *Lyin' Eyes,* are:

City girls just seem to find out early
How to open doors with just a smile

PRO INFO:

- o When you have a record released, you have only a few minutes of air time to capture the attention of the listener.
- o Snare that potential record buyer with a powerful opening statement that will lure him or her into wanting to hear more.
- o Reinforce your lyric with a carefully crafted melodic idea that calls attention to itself.
- o You must strive for second lyrical verses that are stronger than the first to sustain the interest.

ASSIGNMENT

1. Review some of your old songs and evaluate them for the power potential of their opening lines.
2. Create a seductive opening line for one or two of your original titles which you plan to develop into songs at a later time.

Passive listeners must be penetrated. Unsympathetic listeners must be won over, by effective writing, to see your point.

TECHNIQUE #16

Overstating

Lyrics Larger than Life

Exaggeration, unacceptable in normal conversation, is a unique way of packing power into song lyrics. The "larger than life" statement gives emphasis, strength and sincerity to lyrics.

Following is a situation in which a woman, in sheer desperation, is trying to help her inebriated escort out of a panic situation. (The last line says it all.)

The place was in a panic
He had had his twenty rounds
I tried to lift and drag him out
But he weighed *a thousand pounds.*

Descriptive extremes can appear in closing lines, in opening lines, and/or in the body of your lyric.

Overstatements can also be found in song titles. Some make the most fascinating titles:

On a Clear Day You Can See Forever
Fifty Ways to Leave Your Lover
Ain't No Mountain High Enough
Cry Me a River
Fly Me to the Moon

▮ PRO INFO: ▮

An overwhelming statement attracts attention in all forms of communication, written or spoken. These enlargements of life, used thoughtfully and tastefully, can intensify the emotional impact of your song and make it memorable.

The technique: Picture the situation, stretch your imagination, and seek descriptive extremes to make your point.

An entire lyric can be built by creating an overstated, imaginative love song.

Following (recorded with a telegraphic musical background) is an ethereal situation that, in essence, is nothing more than an exaggerated metaphor:

Lyric by Buddy Kaye

Cloud Eight *Calling Cloud Nine*
How are you doing out there?
Are you enjoying the weather?
How would you like to rub our clouds together?

Cloud Eight *Calling Cloud Nine*
Have you made love in mid-air?
It's got to be fun, it's got to be crazy
On a heavenly quilt, warm and lazy

Cloud Eight *Calling Cloud Nine*
—Your cloud or mine?

TECHNIQUE #17

Brevity

The Economy of Language

Although it is advantageous for *statements* to be larger than life, lyrics should, ideally, be short—a few words per line—and be able to stand on their own.

Each line should contain a complete thought.

Whenever possible, each line should *advance* the story.

In the song *The Perfect Woman* (an A–A–B–A song with a two-line extension), observe the economy of language: short lines that stand alone, each containing a complete thought, as each line advances the story.

THE PERFECT WOMAN

Words and Music by
Buddy Kaye and Philip Springer

"A" Finding fault with you
I walked away, said we were through
All to pursue
The perfect woman

"A" Someone who would make
My humdrum life champagne and cake
It just would take
The perfect woman

"B" She'd understand me
My moods wouldn't matter
She'd hand me
The stars on a silver platter

"A" Now that I've been around
I'm back with both feet on the ground
And I have found
The perfect woman

Extension And though I broke every rule
Won't you forgive this perfect fool?

PRO INFO:

The documents that have the greatest effect on humanity are the short ones: eternal quotations from the Bible and Lincoln's monumental Gettysburg Address, which took two minutes to deliver.

Lengthy lines are usually the result of lyrical ideas that ramble. They are not carefully planned and edited, and they often lose the attention of listeners.

Brevity—the technique of using words economically—lets you paint large pictures in a small space.

A love story emotionally involving the lives of three people can be expressed in two simple lines (fourteen words) as in the song *Three's a Crowd*.

I love you . . . and so does he
You're in love . . . but not with me.

The triangle conflict is clearly established. The idea is then completed by the final two lines of the first stanza:

I know two is company
But three's a crowd.

Although brief songs are more difficult to write, they have the dual advantage of being easier to remember and offering greater performance possibilities.

Proof is found in every ball park in America, where thousands join in the rousing eight-line chorus of *Take Me out to the Ball Game*.

Three standouts:

DIDN'T WE

Words and Music by Jimmy Webb
(9 Lines)

This time we almost made the pieces fit, didn't we
This time we almost made some sense of it, didn't we
This time I had the answer right here in my hand
Then I touched it, and it had turned to sand . . .

This time we almost sang the song in tune, didn't we
This time we almost made it to the moon, didn't we
This time we almost made our poem rhyme
And this time we almost made that long, hard climb
Didn't we almost make it this time?

YOU MUST HAVE BEEN A BEAUTIFUL BABY

Lyric by Johnny Mercer
Music by Harry Warren
(10 Lines)

You must have been a beautiful baby
You must have been a wonderful child
When you were only startin' to go to kindergarten
I bet you drove the little boys wild . . .

And when it came to winning blue ribbons
You must have shown the other kids how
I can see the judges' eyes as they handed you the prize
I bet you made the cutest bow
You must have been a beautiful baby
'Cause baby, look at you now

MY FUNNY VALENTINE

Lyric by Lorenz Hart
Music by Richard Rodgers
(11 Lines)

My funny Valentine, sweet comic Valentine
You make me smile with my heart
Your looks are laughable, unphotographable
Yet you're my fav'rite work of art

Is your figure less than Greek?
Is your mouth a little weak?
When you open it to speak—are you smart?

But don't change a hair for me
Not if you care for me
Stay little Valentine, stay
Each day is Valentine's day

PRO INFO:

1. Lyric writing is an exercise in the economy of words.
2. Like a telegram, lyrics should have key words and employ the art of omission.
3. Every lyric line is accountable to the total sum and must therefore be able to stand alone as a complete or connecting thought.
4. Laced with nuances (subtle statements or observations), lyrics have the ability to suggest deeper meanings to sensitive listeners.
5. The ideal playing time for your song is approximately three minutes, including all repetitions. Recording production may increase the length of your song to four minutes, or more.
6. Have your lyrics say all you want to say in a maximum of twenty lines, if possible. There is no rule.
7. Avoid having your lyrics overcrowded with ideas.

The more you say the less people remember.

—FENELON

TECHNIQUE #18

Person-to-Person Lyrics

The "You and Me" Approach

Unless your story connects with life, it doesn't have an impact on anybody. To achieve this impact in a song lyric, it is essential to look for ways to turn your titles and ideas into personalized affirmations, to aim for one-on-one closeness.

Write your lyric as though it were spoken intimately and privately to another person. The listener will find him- or herself in direct touch and accept your song as a personal conversation meant exclusively for him or her.

Personalizing a problem creates an emotional tug. The following four lines from the Eagles' hit *The Best of My Love* effectively create the desired emotional reaction:

Every morning I wake up and worry
What's gonna happen today
You see it your way and I see it mine
But we both see it slippin' away

The intimacy of the "you and me" level of writing draws a greater response than songs which are based on philosophy, grievances, social concerns, or self-pity.

However, personal songs should not have private meanings. Although private meanings are intimate, they usually do not render a broad message and thus defeat the purpose of commercial writing.

One song that achieved the objective of personally affecting listeners is *I Will Survive*.

Careful study of the lyric is suggested. It is a perfect lyric: emotional, meaningful lines, pure rhymes, visual language, contemporary phrases, and very personal. The music is extraordinary.

I WILL SURVIVE

Words and Music by Dino Fekaris and Freddie Perren

At first I was afraid, I was petrified;
Kept thinking I could never live without you by my side.
But then, I spent so many nights thinkin'
How you did me wrong, and I grew strong,
And I learned how to get along.
And so you're back from outer space.
I just walked in to find you here with that sad look upon your face.
I should have changed that stupid lock,
I should have made you leave your key,
If I'd've known for just one second you'd be back to bother me.

Go on now, go walk out the door;
Just turn around, now, 'cause you're not welcome anymore.
Weren't you the one who tried to hurt me with goodbye?
Did you think I'd crumble, did you think I'd lay down and die.
Oh no, not I, I will survive.
For as long as I know how to love, I know I'll stay alive.
I've got all my life to live.
I've got all my love to give and I'll survive.
I will survive.

It took all the strength I had not to fall apart;
Kept tryin' to mend the pieces of my broken heart.
And I spent, oh, so many nights
Just feelin' sorry for myself,
I used to cry, but now I hold my head up high.
And you see me, somebody new.
I'm not that chained up little person still in love with you.
And so you felt like droppin' in
And just expect me to be free,
Well, now, I'm savin' all my lovin' for someone who's lovin' me.

(Repeat chorus)

FIRST, SECOND, AND THIRD PERSONS:

- Begin by creating your synopsis (*Technique #2*) in first person, using the "you and I, you and me" approach.
- *Second person* is directed to another person—"you." (The second person is always the person spoken to.)
- Writing in *third person*—"him," "her," "they" and "them" should be your least used lyrical approach—unless it is the only way your lyric can be effective. (The third person is always the person spoken about.) In this form, you are the narrator.

Every song I sing is part of a conversation between you and me. We've been friends for a long time, sharing all those special feelings through a song. Without someone to listen, there wouldn't be any reason for what I do. When you hear a new song, and it feels like I'm singing right to you, it's because I am.

—Conway Twitty

TECHNIQUE #19

Changing Lyrical Scenes

Creating Visual Excursions

The most interesting lyrics take listeners on *visual excursions.* The use of this technique moves characters from one interesting situation into another. More importantly, it adds story variation when your lyric is in need of a refreshing lift.

The following are some classic songs and hit recording artists that have used this process:

Lucille (Kenny Rogers)—takes the listener from a Toledo barroom to a rented hotel room.

I Do It For Your Love (Paul Simon)—moves the young couple from the marriage license bureau to a small, cold apartment, to buying a rug at a junk shop, then home again.

By the Time I Get to Phoenix (Glen Campbell)—continues to Albuquerque, Oklahoma, and points east.

Rhinestone Cowboy (Glen Campbell)—transplants the main character from the dirty sidewalks of

> Broadway to his fantasy of a star-spangled
> rodeo arena.

Again, this technique is not a *must* for every lyric. Its function is to avoid repetitive details when going from verse to verse in the popular A–B–A–B format.

It allows the lyricist to present a *new angle* of thought in Verse 2, rather than repeat the information previously revealed in Verse 1.

A short lyric example of changing scenes from verse to verse in a country song:

TENNESSEE GIRLS

By Buddy Kaye

Verse 1: (A)	My mother always told me I'd wed a girl from Tennessee And sure enough it happened The way my mother said to me
"Hook" Chorus: (B)	Those Tennessee girls are awfully pretty And I got me one Don't plan on takin' her to the city We're having too much fun
Verse 2: (A)	I once went to a Gypsy Who read my tea leaves in the tea And sure enough she told me I'd wed a girl from Tennessee
"Hook" Chorus: (B)	Those Tennessee girls are awfully pretty And I got me one Don't plan on takin' her to the city We're having too much fun

▌PRO INFO:▐

- Like stage plays, some songs work best in one "set"; others need the added interest of changing scenes to avoid monotony.
- Changing scenes may mean moving into different time periods, recalling other days, inserting flashbacks, introducing a new character in your story, or depicting an unexpected turn of events.
- Changing scenes can add new color and dimension to the subject and sustain interest in the storyline if your lyric calls for it.
- This technique should be kept in mind when formulating the synopsis (*Technique #2*) of your lyric.

TECHNIQUE #20

Prosody

The "Marriage" of Words and Music

Prosody, a word of Greek origin, is defined in songwriting terminology as "the marriage of words and music."

The blending of feeling, style, and substance of words and music is achieved in four categories of writing formats:

1. *Music in search of a lyric*—a situation in which the melody is composed in its entirety and the lyricist is obligated to create a title, idea, and words for the music. Accomplishment of this, at a high level of writing, is probably the most difficult assignment in songwriting.
2. *Lyric in search of a melody*—a situation in which words are written on their own, as one would write a poem, in the hope of inspiring mood-matching music. Although it is less difficult to write music to existing words, a completed lyric does lock the melody writer into a rigid format, allowing no room for musical innovations. In many instances, composers will alter the melody when a better musical phrase presents itself, forcing the lyricist to make word adjustments. These liberties are normal procedure among professional songwriting teams.
3. *Writing words and music, line by line*—a situation in which a writer of both words and music creates from pure inspiration, working from line to line until the song is finished. Writing both words and music effectively poses a

dual responsibility calling for deep concentration to achieve all the elements of a well-crafted song. This system produces *few* completed songs and is not recommended for most songwriters.

4. *Presenting title and some lyric lines to composer.* This approach establishes the "feel" and suggests the tempo of the song that is to be written. The conscientious lyricist is supported by a synopsis, a three-minute movie theme and a list of associated words. (See *Techniques #2, #3,* and *#4.*) The words can create melodic inspiration. Both writers can enjoy artistic freedom on their way toward achieving the perfect marriage of words and music. *This is the recommended procedure for writing songs.*

EXAMPLES OF EFFECTIVE PROSODY

1. *We Are the World (We Are the Children).* Written by Lionel Richie and Michael Jackson to raise money for famine relief in Africa, this inspired gospel mode of words and music touched the hearts of millions. The soulful music expressed the outcry of the lyric to make it the perfect song for the purpose of creating huge record sales.

2. *Raindrops Keep Falling on My Head.* The Hal David lyric provides light, good humor while the Burt Bacharach music bounces along with the imagined rhythm of a windshield wiper on a rainy day.

3. *Up, Up and Away.* The soaring energy of this song by Jim Webb creates an exhilarating feeling of "taking off" into the wild blue yonder. The sensitive listener shares the magical flight.

The great songs of all time are illustrations of prosody at its best. All the elements of the songs are harmoniously saying the identical thing. Take time out to think about these extraordinary blendings of words and music.

Jingle Bells
Easter Parade
Ave Maria
White Christmas
Old Man River
Over There

PRO INFO:

- The art of prosody can only be cultivated by being highly conscious of its existence and its importance.
- Constantly review popular hit songs in which, you believe, the words and music fit hand-in-glove. Learn by example!
- A colleague, John Braheny, summarized this concept with his statement: "You don't want your words to say 'higher and higher' while the music is going lower and lower."

Beyond the Twenty Techniques

In this fascinating profession of word engineering and musical expression, inspiration alone will normally not give you a first-rate finished song. Inspiration is the *beginning* of the songwriting process. It will provide a burst of random lyric lines, disconnected thoughts, and snatches of melodies, but you are still a distance from the finish line.

True, on rare occasions, sudden bursts of inspiration can deliver a complete song which becomes bankable with minor revisions. Those are golden moments, but not dependable.

> Inspiration is an occasional friend:
> Skill is a lifetime ally.

The music industry rewards generously those who can repeatedly prove that they have mastered the craft. The Twenty Techniques are provided for such mastery.

But the techniques are only *tools*. Your own way with words, your experiences and observations are the *roots* of your creativity. In essence, your songs are an extension of yourself—capsuled autobiographies!

The following country music section and sixteen Song-Topics of information are provided to assist you in going beyond the mechanics of the art and craft of songwriting. When the basic mechanics are second nature to you, your creative writing has been freed so that you can concentrate and plan strategies to develop your product.

COUNTRY SONGS

Country Songs

Life Set to Music

While self-contained rock groups provide the vast amount of message, soul, and dance music, more and more people are turning to country music for songs they can sing.

There is hardly a city in the United States today that doesn't have a country music radio station, yet it wasn't too long ago when country music stayed exclusively in the country. The growing importance of these rich tapestries of phraseology in today's market is evidenced by their appearance at the top of all the major pop music charts.

The great appeal for country songs is that they tell stories about people. They are straightforward, sincere, crystal clear in meaning, singable, and memorable.

SUBJECTS AND THEMES OF COUNTRY SONGS

- Unrequited (given but not returned) love
- Lost innocence—fooled by being gullible and naive
- Virtues of true love and marriage
- Faith in the Lord

OTHER COMMERCIAL TOPICS

- Barrooms and drinking
- Cheating and regrets
- Trucking and highway patrols
- Cowboys and rodeos
- Fast cars, jail houses, and fun, fun, fun.

Country songs may have offbeat titles such as:

Tennessee Flat Top Box
Whoever Turned Her On Forgot to Turn Her Off
Don't the Girls Look Prettier at Closing Time?
Y'all Come Back Saloon
I'm Gonna Hire a Wino to Decorate Our Home
All My Ex's Live in Texas

Some are songs with sexual connotations:

You'd Make an Angel Want to Cheat
Behind Closed Doors
Doesn't Anybody Make Love at Home Anymore?
She's Not Really Cheatin' (She's Just Getting Even)
If I Said You Had a Beautiful Body, Would You Hold It Against Me?

REGIONAL SONGS

These songs are comprised of typical country subjects indigenous to the southern and southwestern regions of the United States. The lyrics, to some extent, have a language of their own. The expressions have a unique flavor, and are not always fully understood by those living in other parts of the country.

Record sales of regional song hits are limited in number because, as explained, this style of music does not have the benefit of airplay throughout the United States.

Occasionally, regional songs are so well crafted and their subjects so interesting that they automatically attract national attention. Deejays everywhere "jump" on the record. These songs are known as "crossover songs."

CROSSOVER SONGS

Crossover country songs have the musical uniqueness and universal lyrical contents to invade the radio stations of cities dominated by rock-and-roll music. With increased radio play and a wider audience of record buyers, record sales have been known to triple and quadruple those of the normal regional hits.

Crossover country songs can also find an audience of record buyers overseas, adding immeasurable profits to the bottom line.

Focusing on the lyrics of some of the most successful songs in this group will help you to familiarize yourself with the writing style and subject matter that transcends the country market. (The artist or group who had the hit record is in parentheses.)

The Gambler (Kenny Rogers)
Blue Bayou (Linda Ronstadt)
You Needed Me (Anne Murray)
Ode to Billy Joe (Bobbie Gentry)
She Believes in Me (Kenny Rogers)
I Can't Stop Loving You (Ray Charles)

Harper Valley PTA (Jeanne C. Riley)
The Devil Went Down to Georgia (Charlie Daniels Band)

OUTSTANDING COUNTRY LYRICS

THE WIND BENEATH MY WINGS

By Larry Henley and Jeff Silbar

Verse 1: It must have been cold there in my shadow
To never have sunlight on your face.
You've been content to let me shine.
You always walked a step behind.

Verse 2: I was the one with all the glory,
While you were the one with all the strength
Only a face without a name,
I never once heard you complain

Chorus: Did you ever know that you're my hero,
And everything I'd like to be?
I can fly higher than an eagle
'Cause you are the wind beneath my wings.
You are the wind beneath my wings.

Verse 3: It might have appeared to go unnoticed,
But I've got it all here in my heart

I want you to know I know the truth;
I would be nothing without you

(Repeat chorus)

GEORGIA IN A JUG

(Recorded by Johnny Paycheck)
Words and Music by Bobby Braddock

Verse 1: Mason jars on the dresser filled with quarters and dollars
Savin' 'em for a trip around the world
But now you've changed your tune
There'll be no honeymoon
So tonight I'm going there without you, girl

Chorus: I'm going down to Mexico in a glass of tequila
Going down to Puerto Rico in a bottle of rum
Going out to Honolulu in a Mai-Tai mug
Then I'm coming back home to Georgia in a jug

Verse 2: We'll never ride that bus to Mexico City, it's a pity
We'll never sail our ship into San Juan
You'll never walk with me
On the beach at Waikiki
And we'll never share that brick suburban home.

Extension: Today I'm taking that money out of the jar
Tonight I'll buy my ticket at the corner bar.

(Repeat chorus)

IN REAL LIFE

(Recorded by Ed Hunnicutt)
Words and Music by Kent Robbins

Verse 1: In the movies the heartbreak is pretend.
And it will always end in an hour or two.
In a sad song if someone's done you wrong.
Two minutes and the pain is gone
'Cause it was just a song.

Chorus: But in real life it almost never ends
Though time and friends try to pull you through
In real life sometimes it's the bad dream that
comes true
I know because in real life I lost you.

Verse 2: In a good book the ones that sell the best
Love withstands the test and tears are soon forgot
And on TV goodbye is just a show
Some soap opera writer wrote
He can make pain come and go.

(Repeat chorus)

HAPPY BIRTHDAY, DEAR HEARTACHE

(Recorded by Barbara Mandrell)
Words and Music by Mack David and Archie Jordan

"A" It's just a year today
One year since he went away
So happy birthday, dear heartache
You're one year old today.

"A" There'll be a cake tonight
One candle I will light
So, happy birthday, dear heartache
Old love still burns tonight.

"B" When he walked out I felt my heart break
That's when you came to me dear heartache
You made my heart your home
Now look how big you've grown.

"A" Looks like each guest is here
The blues, the mem'ries, and the tears
So happy birthday, dear heartache
Same time, same place, next year.

I DON'T REMEMBER LOVING YOU

(Recorded by John Conlee)
Words and Music by Harlan Howard and Bobby Braddock

"A" I don't remember loving you
And I don't recall the things you say you put me through
You tell me that you've had a guilty conscience for so long
You say that you walked out on me, you say you did me wrong
Well I just don't see how that could be true
'Cause I don't remember loving you.

"A" I don't remember loving you
I heard you mention children, did you say there's one or two?
You say I quit my job then I drank myself insane

You say that I ran down the highway screaming out your name
That's not the sort of thing that I would do
No, I don't remember loving you.

"A" I don't remember loving you
You might talk to my doctor, he drops by each day at two
I get a funny feeling when I look into your eyes
There's something in your smile that gives my stomach butterflies
You must look like someone I once knew
But I don't remember loving you.

"A" I don't remember loving you
I absolutely positively know it can't be true
But everyone I know here in this place is very strange
If you'll hand me my crayons I'll be glad to take your name
In case I run across the guy you knew
But I don't remember loving you.

GUIDELINES FOR WRITING COUNTRY SONGS

1. Start with a provocative idea or use an uncommon word seldom found in song titles (as in *You Decorated My Life*).
2. Prepare a clear storyline in the form of a synopsis. When you start to write, use simple, everyday language to achieve natural, conversational expressions (see *Technique #13—Language Tone*).

3. Word-paint your story in lyrical pictures. Work in imagery familiar to people in all walks of life.
4. Set your lyric to music that is simple, natural, and even somewhat familiar in sound without being a carbon copy of a current or recent hit on the country charts. Musical innovations should take a "half-step" forward rather than seek new horizons.
5. Convey sincerity and truth when you are writing a ballad. Emotional lines that "hurt" have the greatest impact.
6. Be outrageous when you are writing humorous songs. Let your imagination soar, but keep the lyrics homespun.
7. Always write with a specific recording artist in mind, unless you are writing for yourself as a writer-performer.
8. Writing for a specific artist requires the study of his or her previous hits for style and subject matter.
9. Quoting Aaron Lathan, screenwriter of *Urban Cowboy,* "Country music is the city cowboy's bible, his literature, his self-help book, his culture. It tells him how to live and what to expect."
10. Take the advice of Larry Butler, famous country producer of *The Gambler* (recorded by Kenny Rogers): "One of the best learning lessons for a songwriter can be had for the investment of a few dollars. Buy the number-one single record. Carefully listen to it and in your own handwriting, copy the lyric, line by line, concentrating on form, content, rhyme, style, and country expressions."

PROFESSIONAL INSIGHTS INTO SIXTEEN SONGTOPICS

SONGTOPIC #1

Impact of Lyrics

Verbalizing the Melody

Although music has its own rhythmic and emotional values, it is the lyric of the song that gives drama and impact and meaning to the sounds. Thoughts, ideas, and well-turned phrases, well-crafted, add greatly to the pleasure of listening. Without lyrics, all we can do is hum.

The facts are these: Of the one hundred hit songs on the *Billboard* chart, there are, at the most, only one or two recordings without lyrics. These occasional hit records are called "instrumentals." The recordings feature musical instruments, not voices. And it is for this reason that major music publishers and record executives insist on examining the lyric content before expressing interest in listening to an entire song.

STANDARD SONGS

When standard songs are successfully revived, the style of the music is often changed to meet the current "sound" of the market. However, the words remain exactly as they were written ten, twenty, thirty, forty years ago. And when singers interpret standard songs, they may change notes and chords, and add musical phrases of their own, but the one element they never alter is the lyric.

CHANGES

Rock music does not depend on or demand traditionally articulate lyrics. Its commercial power is based on electronically created sounds: synthesizers, computerized percussion, pushbutton recording studios, and a host of new inventions that eliminate the live musician altogether or add innumerable sound effects to traditional instruments.

Most contemporary records are made for dancing, not singing. Few lasting hit songs have emerged from records that were made just for dancing.

CONTEMPORARY LYRICS

Many contemporary lyricists have turned their backs on the Establishment. The "new" lyrics, sometimes vague and loosely crafted, are vastly different from the Tin Pan Alley code of pure rhyme, exact meter and syllables, and precise, unmistakable meaning in each line. (This style of standard structure has delivered many of the world's greatest popular songs—and still does.)

By being loose, today's lyrics have found new ways to say old things. But lack of structure, required for longevity and reproduction, is often missing in many of the current songs.

What we are hearing are "dreamscapes," impressions of thoughts and feelings in a free form of uninhibited expressions. In essence, the broad strokes taken by new lyricists give record listeners the opportunity to draw their own conclusions about what the lyricist is trying to say.

Self-contained rock groups with their built-in writers, recording without supervisory constraint, have not actually broken old songwriting rules that were the pillars of Tin Pan Alley; they simply ignore them. The accent is on sound. The trade refers to this form of Top 40 creativity as "writing a record" rather than writing a song.

ORIGINAL LYRICS

Just because you have written a lyric or a complete song does not necessarily mean that you have created an *original* work. The dictionary definition of *original* is "that which has *not* been made, done, thought of, or used before."

An imitation of a song that has been a hit is rarely appreciated by professional music people; conversely, the writer of an inspired, inventive idea is applauded and rewarded with overwhelming demands for material from record company executives, producers, and Top 40 artists.

What is considered unique in the song world? The following songs and the artists who made them popular (among many others):

Vincent (Don McLean)
Like a Rolling Stone (Bob Dylan)
Is That All There Is? (Peggy Lee)
King of the Road (Roger Miller)
Spanish Harlem (Ben E. King)
Tie a Yellow Ribbon Round the Old Oak Tree (Tony Orlando)

HOW DO YOU TEST YOUR LYRICS FOR CLARITY?

Ask for feedback from people whose opinions you trust—those who have the ability to listen, the sensitivity to evaluate, and the patience to concentrate and read between the lines.

While some abstract lyrics consist of flamboyant sentences laced with decorative adjectives and flowery phrases, a more controlled writing approach is desirable.

Studying the elements of successful songs can greatly accelerate learning the fine points of the songwriting craft as demanded by the current market. An excellent example of controlled contemporary lyrics is reflected in a song emerging as a new standard, *Year of the Cat*. The recording, by Al Stewart, is available in the larger record shops in major cities.

Following is the lyric:

THE YEAR OF THE CAT

Words and Music by Al Stewart and Peter Wood

"A" On the mornin' from a Bogart movie
In a country where they turn back time
You go strolling through the crowd
Like Peter Lorre contemplating a crime
She comes out of the sun in a silk dress
Running like a watercolor in the rain
Don't bother asking for explanations
She'll just tell you that she came
In the Year of the Cat

"A" She doesn't give you time for questions
As she locks up your arm in hers

And you follow till your sense of which direction
Completely disappears
By the blue-tiled walls near the market stalls
There's a hidden door she leads you through
These days she says I feel my life
Just like a river running through
The Year of the Cat

"B" She looks at you so coolly
And her eyes shine like the moon in the sea
She comes in incense and patchouli
So you take her to find out what's waiting
Inside the Year of the Cat

"A" Well, morning comes and you're still with her
And the bus and the tourists are gone
And you've thrown away your choice
And lost your ticket so you have to stay on
But the drumbeat strains of the night remain
In the rhythm of the newborn day
You know sometime you're bound to leave her
But for now you've got to stay
In the Year of the Cat
In the Year of the Cat

TECHNICAL REVIEW OF *YEAR OF THE CAT*

Technique

#1—*Title:* Original, definitely unique.
#2—*Synopsis:* Interesting, different.
#3—*Three-Minute Movie:* Visually exotic, intriguing conclusion.

#5—*Form:* A–A–B–A.
#6—*Title Repetition:* Well-placed and unmistakable.
#10—*Specifics:* Artful, exotic.
#11—*Imagery:* Rich, colorful.
#13—*Language Tone:* Consistent.
#14—*Emotional Values:* Somewhat aloof, but warm and firm.
#15—*Opening Lines:* Extraordinarily original.
#17—*Brevity:* Big story in small space.
#19—*Changing Lyrical Scenes:* Effective, vivid changes.
#20—*Prosody:* Perfect marriage of words and music beautifully blended in contemporary style.

SONGTOPIC #2

The Inner Lyric

Writing from Within

Songs that emerge as being the most meaningful to an audience are those that capture a slice of life—preferably your own!

Each writer has his or her own way of reaching inward. By opening your eyes to observe and then closing them to reflect, you allow your reflections to transfer themselves into feelings. Your feelings become inspired words. The inner lyric, when allowed to surface, will be strongly felt and totally honest.

REFLECTIVE WRITING

Reflective writing consummates itself in the art of sharing your inner world with the outside world. One can think of this as a kind of spiritual experimentation. Tapping the resources of your inner self can be the beginning of enlightenment, both as a writer and as a person.

PRO INFO:

- Don't think! Feel!
- The inner lyric can add to the believability of love songs.
- Uninhibited truth and sincerity are the components that produce meaningful lyrics.
- Write your feelings down on paper before you edit them in your mind.
- There are no new story plots. It's a matter of expressing your own experiences in a fresh way.

SOMEONE ELSE'S STORY

Some songwriters find it difficult to reveal their innermost feelings for all the world to hear. This can be the result of personal shyness, among other reasons.

If you find that you are having difficulty in revealing your personal thoughts and feelings, turn your talents to telling the story of someone you know. Empathy is the secret of such writing.

Empathy is the imaginative projection of one's personality into another person. You stop being yourself and become the other person.

The sum total of your own perceptions and experiences, whether real or imagined, will enrich your writings and someone else's story will have its own unique qualities.

Some imagined characters who inspired hit songs are:

Mack the Knife
Delta Dawn
Bad, Bad Leroy Brown

Speedy Gonzales
Mister Bojangles
Coward of the County

Winners or losers, imagined characters have one thing in common—they are always interesting.

SONGTOPIC #3

Discipline

Four Lines a Day

Discipline is the personal drive to practice until you become perfect.

The dedicated songwriter is motivated by the joy of making music. The possibility of making money from music is a secondary consideration. The primary concern should be to master the art.

Writing is like a muscle. It needs daily development. Waiting for inspiration usually creates more waiting. For this reason it is essential that you set time aside, day or night, to do nothing but write.

TALENT IS WASTED WITHOUT DISCIPLINE

The great advantage of steadily and continuously grinding out material is that, when you are ready to make your professional debut, you will have given yourself a wealth of material from which to select your best song.

FOUR LINES A DAY

Here is an easy discipline: Working with one of your titles (*Technique #1*), your synopsis (*Technique #2*), your three-minute movie (*Technique #3*) and associated words (*Technique #4*), give yourself a goal of *four lines a day*—lines that are well thought out and polished. The number of songs you complete will pleasantly surprise you and encourage you to continue this discipline.

Dramatize your feelings—there is no better catharsis.

—OSCAR HAMMERSTEIN II

SONGTOPIC #4

The Power of Words

They sing. They hurt. They sanctify. They were man's first immeasurable feat of magic. They liberated us from ignorance and our barbarous past. For without these marvelous scribbles which build letters into words, words into sentences, sentences into systems and sciences and creeds, man would forever be confined to the self-isolated prison of the cuttlefish or the chimpanzee.

We live by words: LOVE, TRUTH, GOD. We fight for words: FREEDOM, COUNTRY, FAME. We die for words: LIBERTY, GLORY, HONOR. They bestow the priceless gift of articulacy on our minds and hearts—from "Mama" to "infinity." And those who truly shape our destiny, the giants who teach us, inspire us, lead us to deeds of immortality are those who use words with clarity, grandeur and passion: Socrates, Jesus, Luther, Lincoln, Churchill. Americans, caught between affluence and anxiety, may give thanks for the endless riches in the kingdom of print.

This inspiring and dynamic description of "The Power of Words" was written by novelist Leo Rosten.

As a songwriter, transforming raw information into fresh lyrical ideas, it is vital that you develop a sense of drama, poignancy, and joy in your writing.

Your lyrics should be written in contemporary terms, reflecting current vocabulary, colloquialisms, and inoffensive slang.

Although many people consider "street talk" an abuse of language, it is precisely this kind of lyric that creates a familiar bond between a song and its listeners in today's world.

There are fashions in language just as there are fashions in attire. *Groovy, Man, Groovy!* is a classic example of how language changes with the times.

(Author unknown)

Remember when hippy meant big in the hips
And a trip involved travel in cars, planes and ships.
When pot was a vessel for cooking things in
And hooked was what grandmother's rug might have been.

When fix was a verb that meant mend or repair
And be-in meant merely existing somewhere?
When neat meant well-ordered, tidy and clean.
And grass was a ground cover normally green.

When lights and not people, were switched on and off
And the Pill might have been what you took for a cough.
When camp meant to quarter outdoors in a tent
And pop was what the weasel went.

When groovy meant furrowed with channels and hollows
And birds were winged creatures, like robins and swallows.
When fuzz was a substance, real fluffy like lint
And bread came from bakeries, not from the mint.

When square meant a 90-degree angled form
And cool was a temperature not quite warm?
When roll meant a bun, and rock was a stone
And hang-up was something you did with a phone.

When jam was preserves that you spread on your bread
And crazy meant balmy, not right in the head?
When swinger was someone who swung in a swing
And pad was a soft sort of cushiony thing.

When way out meant distant and far, far away
And a man couldn't sue you for calling him gay.

Words once so sensible, sober and serious
Are making the freak scene, like psychodelirious.
It's groovy man, groovy, but English it's not,
Methinks that our language is going to pot.

PRO INFO:

Think of words as bricks with which to build your song lyrics—properly assembled they can become monumental.

Dictionaries contain amazing information in addition to definitions. They increase your word power, indicate accented syllables, trace derivations, and illustrate multiple meanings.

Awareness of the many uses and connotations of the same word gives you the option of writing many different lines. For example, there are some thirty uses and meanings for the word "block":

There's a *city* block, a *butcher* block, an *auction* block, a *hat* block and a *writer's* block.

You can block a *pass,* block out *noise,* block out a *dress* pattern—you can even knock someone's block off.

The word "run" has well over one hundred uses and meanings.

There's a *dog* run, a *stocking* run, and a run for your *money*. You can run an *errand,* run a *blockade,* run a forty-yard *dash,* run an *elevator,* have the run of the *house,* and have a run of good *luck*.

Additionally, there's a run in *cards,* a run in *billiards,* a run in *baseball,* a run on *banks*. You can run up a *hill,* and you can run up a *bill,* and you can feel run *down.* You can run *against time,* and you can physically run *into someone* or have a run-in *with someone.* You can run out of *money* and *ideas.* You run through *music* and *plays.* And you can even run yourself *wild!*

Words are the voice of the heart.

—Confucius

SONGTOPIC #5

The Charisma of Music

Music has the powerful ability to evoke memories. In a matter of a few bars, music can transport you back in time, make you smile, or fill your eyes with tears.

The chromatic musical scale has twelve tones. The music that you create with these twelve notes is an intricate composite of your sensitivity, imagination, and natural talent.

Being a professional musician with knowledge of the wealth of countless chord patterns is a big plus as a melody writer. But it is not essential. If you "feel" music and hear it inside yourself, you can produce beautiful songs without being a musician. There will always be someone who can listen to your song, play it, and notate it.

With few exceptions, the most valuable copyrights (those songs with lasting popularity) are uncomplicated melodies that people can remember easily.

PRO INFO:

Just as the lyricist in a writing team must have an interesting idea for the lyric, so should the music writer have an *idea* for his or her music. Rambling and monotonous melodies are forced to lean heavily on percussion instruments, synthesizers, vocal backgrounds, and so forth, for their commercial life. If they miraculously succeed, their life is short.

Dr. Philip Springer—musician, composer, teacher, and musicologist—gives the following advice on writing the melody line:

> When a melody springs into your mind and you have it safely stored on your cassette, let it ferment and develop. When you get back to it, work diligently to simplify it. Test it by putting it aside for a few days, and if it still sounds good to you when you get back to it again, you can begin to feel that you have composed a piece of music to put your faith in and bank your hopes on. . . .
>
> I urge the new songwriters to study the vital rhythms, melodic simplicity, and harmonic logic of the world's most gifted popular music writers, such as George Gershwin, Richard Rodgers, Harold Arlen, Harry Warren; and also the more contemporary writers, such as Antonio Carlos Jobim, Burt Bacharach, Lionel Richie and Paul McCartney. Familiarizing yourself with the style of successful melody writers, past and present, is essential to the process of strengthening and developing your own style as a contemporary composer.

Commenting on one of the composing styles employed by Richard Rodgers, one of the world's foremost composers, Dr. Springer continues: "In the Richard Rodgers songs, *Where or When* and *If I Loved You,* the melody is played exclusively on the *white keys* in the Key of C (diatonic), but the harmonies in the left hand utilize the *black keys* for exotic coloring (chromatic)."

In other words, the genius of Rodgers's melody writing was that it consisted of embellishing simple melodies with an array of rich, harmonious chords.

Dr. Springer's advice and fascinating discovery are obviously worth your investigation.

In order to compose, all you need is to remember a tune that nobody else has thought of.

—ROBERT SCHUMANN

SONGTOPIC #6

Writing Music to Established Chords

In the Pro Info section of Technique #5, I discussed the practice of writing your own lyric to a melody of a current or standard song. This exercise was established so that new writers could instantly be involved in practicing form, meter, rhyme and construction with professional material. There is a counterpart exercise for music writers.

Using printed sheet music of current or standard hit songs practice the chord progressions by themselves, ignoring the familiar melody. After mentally separating the melody from the chords, set out to write your *own* music to the sequence of chords. There are limitless possibilities when you begin to change note values in each bar as you establish your own original music.

A word of caution: Although chord progressions cannot be copyrighted, similar melodies are illegal, and dishonest to borrow. You can lose most or all of your royalties if you become involved in a plagiarism lawsuit, and pay severe financial penalties as well. Nor can you use any part of a melody to which you write your practice lyric.

TESTING YOUR MELODY

A loosely structured rambling melody that emerges from just humming and strumming on your guitar usually is difficult for anyone but the writer to remember. To know whether you have memorable music, play your tune to your friends. After a few minutes of conversation, ask them to sing the melody back to you. This is another moment of truth the songwriter has to contend with, and the beneficiary is you.

Conversely, a solidly constructed melody has memory power. It has character even when it is played with one finger on the piano or hummed to the mellow chords of a guitar.

Try this one-finger test with some of the tunes that are familiar to you:

If
Alfie
Smoke Gets in Your Eyes
Send In the Clowns
Just the Way You Are
That's What Friends Are For

PRO INFO:

Just as you must diligently hunt for a lyrical idea to say something fresh and different, you must also search for a combination of notes and rhythm patterns emanating from chord progressions you have personally assembled. The deeper your well of musical knowledge, the more innovative will be your creativity and originality, and the more effective your ability to evoke feelings and impressions in listeners.

SONGTOPIC #7

Rewriting

Revisiting Your "Completed" Song

There are many talented songwriters in the world. However, there are few who have the willingness and patience to *write* and *rewrite* in order to extend their talent to the limit.

All songs, regardless of style, require careful writing. Too many new writers find greater satisfaction in completing a song as quickly as possible, rather than as faultlessly as possible.

We discussed the importance of letting your inspiration flow freely and of drawing from within yourself. This is an important function for the writer. But once the first burst of enthusiasm is down on paper, it is essential that you are open to the scrutiny of your own work.

If you fall in love with every lyric line and music note you create, you may bypass the opportunity to replace what you have written with something that can be expressed more effectively, more dynamically.

As you struggle to complete the final touches of your rewrite, it is natural to feel a certain amount of boredom and anxiety. But evaluating and editing your work is critical! The difference is, you can make a "good" song into a "great" song by having the patience and tenacity to fine-tune your original effort.

PRO INFO:

- Complete every song you start.
- When you believe your song is finished, set it aside for a few days. In songwriter's jargon: "Put it on ice."
- Return to your completed words and music with the attitude that it is someone else's song. Now rip into it!
- If what you have written hasn't retained its initial excitement, take the songwriter's "scalpel" to it—make it the song you honestly wanted to hear when you were first inspired to write it.
- The Edisonian approach: If one thing doesn't work, try another. (Thomas Edison experimented with thousands of different materials before he happened upon tungsten to make the filament for the electric light bulb.)

WHEN IS A SONG FINISHED?

"Never!" However, you have to stop writing sometime. You'll instinctively know when to stop if you review your polished song and compare it with the quality of the *best* songs played on the radio. When you honestly feel that your song is as good or better, you have probably reached your artistic limit—this time around.

Following is the initial draft of a lyric that had commercial possibilities, but failed in the actual writing stage—except for one interesting line.

The second draft incorporates that particular line, which becomes the *title* of the new version, using a different approach.

The new title inspired a different form, which was actually closer to what had been originally envisioned, but not achieved.

FIRST DRAFT

A CROWDED ROOM

Lyric by Buddy Kaye

Verse:
No use pretending
I know there's another man
Is it serious . . . I just can't tell
I only know what started out as heaven turned into hell
And it doesn't sit too well . . .

Chorus:
We live in a crowded room
Like birds in a crowded nest
We eat at a crowded breakfast table
With an *uninvited guest*

It's you and me and the other person
You keep thinking of all the time
And it will always be a crowded room
Until he moves out of your mind

(This ungraceful lyric, at best, turned out to be a synopsis for something better. One line was responsible for a complete rewrite, as so often happens when you keep trying.)

SECOND DRAFT

THE UNINVITED GUEST

Lyric by Buddy Kaye
Music by Jeff Tweel

Verse 1: His ghost is there
I can see the outline of his shadow traced in the air
Sometimes I see him bending over your shoulder
I think: "What lies has he told 'er."
And I see a smile light up your face
Like you liked what he said . . .
And I want to cry, "It's killing me,"
But I play dumb instead

Chorus: He's the uninvited guest
Who lives in our house
He's the other man who's on your mind
Who's in your life
I would have to be blind
Not to see it, not to feel it
And I'm running second best
To the uninvited guest
And it's breaking my heart

Verse 2: You don't know I know
If it all was in the open you'd deny that it's so . . .
Just like the old song "Torn Between Two Lovers"
It's not happening to others
It's happening to you and me
And the pain is intense
I should leave you but I love you
Though it doesn't make sense

Chorus: He's the uninvited guest
Who lives in our house

He's the other man who's on your mind
Who's in your life
I would have to be blind
Not to see it, not to feel it
And I'm running second best
To the uninvited guest
And it's breaking my heart

SONGTOPIC #8

Collaboration

Creative Partnerships

In the over one-hundred-year history of popular songwriting, very few professional writers have successfully sustained themselves as writers of both words and music. Each part is so demanding and so specialized that it becomes imperative for each writer to find a partner to enhance the area in which he or she is weaker.

The challenge is for two writers (one strong as a melodist, the other strong as a lyricist) to blend their respective talents into one voice in order to create the perfect "marriage" of words and music.

The desire to have the best words for your music and vice versa should encourage every writer to find equally talented collaborators.

In the major cities this process is usually accomplished by locating songwriting organizations. Los Angeles Songwriters Showcase in Hollywood keeps track of these organizations throughout the United States.

In small cities the most effective way to locate songwriting collaborators is through the medium of advertising: newspapers, bulletin boards, recording studios, musical instruments shops, the music departments of high schools and colleges, and introducing yourself to nightclub musicians.

Collaboration means having a partner so that each can see and approach the writing problem from a different point of view—one searching above, the other searching below; one creating, the other editing.

IDEAS FOR SUCCESSFUL COLLABORATION

- Come in prepared with ideas, titles, melodies, artists for whom to write, and new trends to be discussed.
- Be patient with each other during the creative process. Difference of opinion is the foundation of discovery.
- Be flexible. Avoid stubbornness when changes are suggested. You can always return to the old ideas.
- Avoid working in a distracting environment. Shut off the telephone. Put a "do not disturb" sign on the door of your workroom.
- Sit quietly and think. A calm atmosphere can be productive. Constantly improvising on the piano or guitar, hoping that a melody will magically present itself, is distracting to the lyricist.
- Trust and respect for each other is the essence of true collaboration.
- Finding the common ground of agreement is the ultimate objective of writing partners.

SONGTOPIC #9

Coping with Writer's Block

Writer's block is a term used to describe a time when nothing creative will come to mind. This temporary mental "power failure" may be the result of being physically tired, spiritually uninspired, or just generally frustrated.

Yet the challenge of every songwriter is to develop and emerge. What can you do to activate your mind?

1. Temper your disillusionment when your songs do not measure up to your expectations. Your job is to do the best you can.
2. When you feel a lack of inspiration, put demands on yourself. *Force creativity*. Writing four lines a day may seem a mechanical approach, but it is an excellent discipline.
3. When you reach an *extended* period of being unproductive, list your excuses for not putting the time into writing that you planned to, hoped to, tried to, really wanted to do.
4. The ritual of preparing yourself to write can help get you started. A short nap prior to your evening writing session can restore your energy. Stretching and deep-breathing exercises can invigorate your mind.
5. Eliminate outside distractions prior to writing. Stay calm.

6. If clichés trigger your creative engine, use them as stepping stones to higher levels of creativity.
7. When in the midst of writing you find yourself running out of ideas, take a production break. Change your atmosphere. Walk, read, engage in a ping-pong match, or listen to your favorite music.
8. Draw creativity from the following strategy: Print your favorite titles at the top of blank pages, one title to a page. Review these titles when you are trying to find inspiration. Unfailingly, one title will match your mood and trigger a lyrical flow. Continue with this lyric until you have exhausted your ideas.
9. Collaborate. Turn to a writing partner for inspiration and new vitality.

SONGTOPIC #10

Critiquing Your Own Song

A Rating Method

Evaluating your creative efforts is undoubtedly one of the most trying tasks one can attempt. Some people have a tendency to underrate themselves or their work, while others pin medals on themselves before the full honor is deserved.

Critiquing your own work is especially difficult because you may have learned to cherish each and every word and note of music you have written. In fact, you may be stubbornly reluctant to abandon any of them even if there is the possibility that you will find a more effective way to say the same thing. This attitude is certainly contrary to self-improvement.

The dilemma suggests that we should voluntarily back away from our own creative efforts and, when we return, treat our work as though it belonged to someone else.

Critiquing your own songs takes skill, practice, and knowledge of the best and most popular standard songs to be used as role models. Comparing your work to the very best examples that exist creates a perspective for self-evaluation that is second to none.

Joining a group of songwriters in your area, or forming a group through the placement of flyers in schools, recording studios, and music hangouts can produce opinions that may be more "professional" than those of friends and relatives.

PRO INFO:

- Listen to old, tried-and-true, proven standard songs on the middle-of-the-road radio stations just as ardently as you listen to the new music of the day on rock-oriented stations.
- Composers should familiarize themselves with the original music of Burt Bacharach, Antonio Carlos Jobim, and other contemporary composers, as well as classical composers, for enrichment.
- Study chord progressions and lyrical devices and apply this knowledge to your own works.
- Experiment. Uncharted areas can be rewarding.
- If you write both words and music, always bow to the superior element of your song. Example: If you find a strong melody first, adapt your lyric to it. If you have an outstanding lyric line, adjust the music to fit the words.
- Embrace the experience of the professional (teacher, publisher, artist, producer) who has been trained to evaluate your words and music commercially.
- Accept all criticism professionally, not personally.
- Constantly refine and polish your lyric. Experiment with your music. Remember—what is boring in a lyric is predictability.
- Being totally honest with yourself when you evaluate your work allows you to develop a "rating system" for the songs you write. Using a scale of one to ten, ten being perfect, give your newest effort an overall rating. Put the song aside and then return to it with the idea of revising your work to improve your rating.

The first and final thing you have to do in this world is to last in it and not be smashed by it, and it is the same way with your work.

—Ernest Hemingway

THE BUSINESS OF MUSIC

SONGTOPIC #11

Listener Reactions

Why People Buy Records

Songwriting is a profession in which songwriters produce psychological effects in music that lead to the creation of moods and feelings in listeners. The objective is to crowd people out of their own minds and occupy their space with your song. Therefore, knowing why people react favorably to some songs and not to others is critical to becoming successful in this endeavor, and remaining successful.

The first reaction a listener has to a song is *sound*. Sound, more than any other element, is largely responsible for the success of rock music: a combination of the "beat" enhancing the intense singing style of the lead vocalist of a power-charged group of musicians.

The second is an *emotional* reaction. The listener is lyric-conscious and mood-affected as he or she identifies with the sentiment or situation that the words reveal.

The third is an *intellectual* reaction. The listener is moved by the blending of original music and intelligent words. He or she appreciates phrases of imagery and impressions, and has the ability to read between the lines for nuances and delicate shades of meanings, which are interpreted for their subtleties.

Any one of these three reactions to songs can produce a hit and a record-buying customer. Two levels of positive response increase your chances for a hit. Three levels produce a "can't-miss" hit. Songs in the last category are:

I Believe
Stardust
Born to Run
Windmills of Your Mind
Killing Me Softly with His Song

The game plan for commercial writing is to bring the listeners' senses into play. We know about the five senses human beings enjoy. Music buyers are notorious for having a "sixth sense," which detects the emotional message and forms the overall impression they gather from the song they hear. They can "smell" a hit. The songwriter's job is to supply the aroma.

SONGTOPIC #12

Selling Your Songs

The Professional Way

Whether you send your cassettes to music publishers through the mail after first establishing a contact, or audition your songs in person (which is the most effective way to sell), your preparation should be the same. Here are some ideas:

1. Write every day for the next six months or so, religiously following the concepts of *Method Songwriting*.
2. Use feedback from others, then select and polish your best three songs from the fifteen to twenty songs you should have completed in this time period.
3. Demo these songs in a professional studio, or with professional recording equipment at home, with guitar or piano accompaniment. Quality is essential. Hard rock material should be group demoed in a fashion that is close to recorded songs played on the radio.
4. Type the lyrics clearly, indicating verse, chorus, and so on. Include your name, address, and telephone number.
5. Do business with reputable music publishers only! Beware of any person or company requesting money for *any* reason. The long-established, legitimate music publisher is the best direct contact to a record company.
6. A list of respected music publishers can be found in Nashville, Hollywood, and New York City telephone books

or by contacting Los Angeles Songwriters Showcase. These publishers should *not* be approached until your songs have been evaluated locally and judged to be of high quality in originality and craftsmanship.

7. Copyrighting your songs (words and music) prior to submitting them to a publisher is a personal decision. Some writers mail their songs to themselves via *registered mail.* This establishes priority but is not considered an official copyright. Other writers mail ten, even twenty songs recorded on one cassette to:

Register of Copyrights
Copyright Office
Library of Congress
Washington, D.C. 20559

The fee is ten dollars for the cassette, provided there is one title for all the songs. Example: *John Doe Medley.*

The Copyright Office also supplies free forms, called *Form PA,* for published and unpublished songs. It is advisable to write for Circular R50 for general information prior to registering your song.

WARNING: Do *not* under any circumstances send your lyric to a "song shark." A song shark is an individual or a company that charges *you* a fee to publish *your* lyric. These sharks advertise in the classified sections of many magazines; they promise to take your lyric and set it to music, copyright your lyric, even record your song. It's a ripoff designed to extract money from you, not to help you break in to the business of songwriting. Ignore such advertisements, and approach only legitimate music publishers with your work.

SONGTOPIC #13

How to Cast Your Song for a Recording Artist

The song may be the "thing," but getting it recorded is everything! Intelligent casting is critical.

1. If you are *not* writing songs for your own gratification, you should be writing for artists currently on the record charts, molding every lyric line and musical phrase to fit the specific style of the recording artist in mind.
2. Whether you are submitting your songs to a professional music publisher or pursuing the recording artist on your own, it is advantageous to know *when* the artist is scheduling a recording session, and what musical direction he or she is considering.
3. This information is available via "tip sheets" published in Hollywood, Nashville, and New York City. Songwriters Guild of America in New York, and Los Angeles Songwriters Showcase and National Academy of Songwriters in Hollywood can provide current "tip sheet" subscription information.
4. Getting your song recorded is a combination of having the right song and contacting the right artist at the right time. Being somewhat familiar with the life style of the artist can alleviate some of the guesswork of delivering the right songs.

One of the things to consider is subject matter. For example, if a recording artist has been divorced for the second or third time, you wouldn't want to hand him a song called *You Only Love Once*. On the other hand, if a performer is known to be happily married, she wouldn't be interested in a song called *Love Is for the Birds*.

RULE #1: COLLECT DETAILS

The first rule in casting is to collect small details about an artist's life style, philosophies, habits, and hobbies, and to keep up with the changes as they occur.

Information about recording artists can be found in song lyric magazines, newspaper articles, music trade papers, and sometimes can be heard on radio and TV interviews.

In a general business sense, your chances of pleasing a performer are enhanced when the artist hears a song lyric that parallels his or her own thinking.

Following is a personal incident that helped me create a lyric for a famous recording artist. The person was being interviewed by a TV host. Among other things, she spoke of a recent dark period in her life. When she was asked if she felt that her career was over, she raised her voice and haughtily exclaimed, "Hell, no! I'm just gettin' started."

With my writing notebook close at hand, I hurriedly picked up a pen. The lines of the lyric poured out spontaneously. I was inspired! I had heard something in the interview that triggered a creative response. Here was a determined lady about to make a comeback in life. I *knew* I could write her story.

JUST GETTIN' STARTED

Lyric by Buddy Kaye
Music by Chuck Sabatino

Verse 1: I've been thru heaven, I've been thru hell
Now I'm doin' my best to stay somewhere between
You took me thru changes, too many to tell
But I've learned a lot from what I've heard and seen.

I'm talkin' to you, life . . . so hear what I say
You thought I was thru, life . . . well, there ain't no way.

Chorus: I'm just gettin' started
I got a lot of time on my side
I'm just gettin' started
There's still a lot of road left to ride
I'm going forward, not looking back
Gave up for a minute, now I'm on the attack.
I'm just gettin' started
Hello, new day
Here I come . . . get out of my way.

Verse 2: I've had the good times, I've had it bad
Guess I wrote my own ticket to ev'ry place I've been
Some gave me something, some took all I had
And it all was goin' down like nasty gin.

I'm talkin' to you, life . . . 'cause I'm feelin' strong
You thought I was thru, life . . . well, you read me wrong.

Chorus: I'm just gettin' started
I gotta lot of time on my side

I'm just gettin' started
There's still a lot of road left to ride
I'm going forward, not looking back
Gave up for a minute now I'm on the attack
I'm just gettin' started
Hello, new day
Here I come . . . get out of my way

RULE #2: IDENTIFY RECEPTIVE PERFORMERS

As you know, many performers write their own songs. It is therefore incumbent upon you to do your homework before casting your songs. Review record labels for writer credits. If the songwriters are people other than the recording artist(s), the chances are that you are not wasting time in submitting your songs.

Following are some of the prominent recording names who collaborate with other writers and accept outside material:

Quincy Jones
Sheena Easton
Barry Manilow
Glen Campbell
Linda Ronstadt
Barbra Streisand
Ronnie Milsap
The Pointer Sisters
Olivia Newton-John

RULE #3: LEARN FROM HISTORY

Review previous hit songs associated with each recording artist. Study the style of music. For instance, does the artist prefer upbeat dance music or old-style ballads? Should the "flavor" of the song be pop, adult-oriented, teenage, country, hard rock, blues, or R & B (rhythm and blues).

Review the artist's preferences in subject matter: "sad" songs, "hurt" songs, stories about other people, barroom ballads, or bedroom songs.

Decide whether the lyrics should be expressed intellectually or in country jargon; in street talk or pillow talk; in lyrical sensitivity or driving repetition.

Review the vocal range of the artist. Does he or she sound best in the lower or higher range of the music scale? Some famous recording artists cannot vocally stretch beyond twelve tones on the piano scale. Others glide through a two-octave range with the greatest of ease.

The *number-one criterion* in casting your song is that it is indeed a song—a solid, well-thought-out memorable melody with meaningful words rather than an average, so-so effort heavily dependent on rhythmic factors and high-tech sounds to make it a hit song. This, in songwriter's jargon, is called "writing a record."

Ron Miller, the outstanding lyricist of the Stevie Wonder classic *For Once in My Life,* summed it up this way: "Writing a 'record' can make money. Writing a song can give you a career."

The business of songwriting supports the theory that what you don't know *can* hurt you.

SONGTOPIC #14

Ten "Don'ts" When You're with a Music Publisher

If you are presenting your songs in person, the following is a list of "don'ts":

1. *Don't* start explaining what the song is about, or why you wrote it, how much time you put into it, how great your friends think it is. Just play the song.
2. *Don't* make excuses for a poor demo, inferior home recording equipment, the fact that the background is drowning out the lead vocal. Avoid these problems in the first place.
3. *Don't* present songs that you haven't tested with impartial listeners. Your reputation is on the line, even if you wrote only part of the song. Each cowriter is responsible for the whole.
4. *Don't* begin your song with a long instrumental introduction. Avoid long musical interludes between verses and choruses. Four-bar intros are perfect. Publishers are impatient people.
5. *Don't* present handwritten or handprinted lyrics to a publisher. Have your lyric typed neatly.
6. *Don't* take an ordinary song to a publisher and explain how great it will sound when it is recorded with a full battery of musicians. If the song you are demonstrating does not move the publisher, it will never get into the recording studio.

7. *Don't* present more than three songs at one time. Be sure to have two others with you—the publisher may want to listen to other songs you have written.
8. *Don't* show a song that is a copycat, follow-up version of a current hit. If a publisher wants more of the same, he will go back to the original writer.
9. *Don't* ask a publisher for feedback, such as what he liked and didn't like about your song. He may volunteer suggestions for small changes. However, he is not there to be your teacher and may even resent being pushed for comments.
10. *Don't* defend your work. Don't hard sell or argue in its favor if you receive a rejection. This will just close the door for your next visit. Simply say, "Thank you for listening. I hope I can come by again." This response indicates a professional attitude.

For a further understanding of the business side of songwriting, read *This Business of Music,* a comprehensive 595-page guide to the music industry by Sidney Shemel and M. William Krasilovsky, published in New York City by Billboard Publications. The study of this work should only be attempted by the serious songwriter who wishes to delve deeply into the domestic and foreign business aspect of the trade.

Under normal circumstances, if your song is published by a major music publisher, that publisher will be familiar with the information required to protect the songwriter throughout the world.

SONGTOPIC #15

Dealing with Criticism

Rising Above the Negatives

All creative efforts are subject to criticism. If we are attempting to write for the commercial marketplace, we must be ready to accept comments that may hurt our feelings.

Some critics are better, sharper, and more articulate than others. Look for those who are specific and can be clear and constructive as to why they like or don't like your songs.

Don't fall into the trap of thinking someone is a good critic just because he or she always agrees with you. You should become suspicious if someone loves everything you write. Families and close friends have this tendency.

Collecting many opinions will lead you to the right decision.

Although it is in your best interest to weigh every "improvement" carefully, you should be warned that if you listen to what everyone says, you might find yourself losing your own style and writing everyone else's song.

We think too small. Like the frog at the bottom of the well. He thinks the sky is only as big as the top of the well. If he surfaced, he would have an entirely different view.

—Mao Tse-tung

SONGTOPIC #16

Winning

Counting on Yourself

Songwriting is a personal, highly individual profession. In time, almost every writer finds his or her own way to create songs and make them available to the public.

Guidance from music publishers, record companies and theatrical agents is not usually available. Publishers' reps look for polished, professional demos they can enthusiastically submit to recording artists and record producers after the first hearing.

Although you will undoubtedly learn more from success, you first must learn to accept the lessons of failure. But if you love songwriting enough, you will find most obstacles are far less important than they appear to be.

Judging from the rapid erosion of many contemporary hit songs, it appears that the public can be comfortable with mediocrity. It is therefore important that you realize that the Top 40 songs do not always make it to the top of the charts because they are *great* songs. The popularity of a group or performer frequently determines the popularity of a song.

The job of the serious songwriter is to write each song better than the one before. In doing so, keep in mind that the struggle encountered in the development of the tools of the craft is a necessary part of the learning process.

And if ever your spirits need a lift, you might turn to The Songwriter's Survival Kit on the following page. It was created to be your friend.

The Songwriter's Survival Kit

- *Set a well-defined goal for yourself.* Example: Write every day.
- *Don't be impatient.* Don't set a time limit on your progress and your ultimate success.
- *Be honest with yourself.* Ask yourself with every song you are about to write: What is the point I want to make? Is what I am about to say important?
- *Strive for originality.* You will be noticed.
- *Be industrious.* Complete every assignment that you give yourself.
- *Believe in yourself.* Believe in your ability to develop and emerge.
- *Reach for your competitive fire.* This will motivate you in writing, revising, demonstrating, and selling your songs.
- *Strive for excellence.* Never settle for mediocrity.

When love and skill come together, expect a masterpiece.

ADDENDA

ADDENDUM #1

Subjects to Write About

A song being played on the air has only a few minutes to attract and impress the potential record-buying customer. And every second counts!

The choice of subject and how to express it are vital decisions for commercially minded songwriters.

A great deal of care must be used in choosing the *right subject* for a song. Recording artists are very protective of their public image and won't sing about controversial subjects. Like the consumer, artists look for honesty, sincerity, and innovation in their songs.

The following pages present the ten most popular categories of subjects to write about. Topics with the broadest appeal are:

1. Love Songs
2. "Laundry List" Songs
3. Current News, Trends, and Message Songs
4. Personal Experiences
5. Novelty Songs
6. Name Songs
7. Character Songs
8. Story Songs
9. Motion Picture Titles
10. Special Situation Songs

LOVE SONGS

There are different kinds of love songs because of the different kinds of love that we experience. Some examples follow:

1. The conventional love songs—Whitney Houston singing: *Didn't We Almost Have It All* and *Saving All My Love for You.*
2. The mother and child love song, as in: *You and Me Against the World.*
3. The father and child love song: *Daddy Don't You Walk So Fast* and *Watching Scotty Grow.*
4. The insecure love song, as in: *Will You Love Me Tomorrow?*
5. The love song of frustration: *Just Once.*
6. The hopeful love ballad, as in: *The Old Songs.*

Warm, carefully crafted love songs appeal to the broadest audience and therefore enjoy the longest life. Because of their uncompromising demand for utter simplicity, sincerity and originality, love songs are probably the most difficult to write.

It is said that it is easier to write from anger than from love!

"LAUNDRY LIST" SONGS

The "laundry list" song is a Tin Pan Alley innovation that has absolutely nothing in common with what the name implies. A "laundry list" song is simply one that makes its point by listing various objects, places, or situations.

Some famous songs in this category are:

Thanks for the Memory
Fifty Ways to Leave Your Lover
You're Moving Out Today

An innovative example of the "Laundry List" was the use of the 26 letters in the alphabet: "A—You're Adorable, B—You're so Beautiful. . . ," right through X, Y, Z.

One brilliant example of this approach to lyric writing which incorporates overstatement at its best (*Technique #16*) is Cole Porter's song *You're the Top*—positive proof that you can make your point with a "Laundry List" and be entertaining at the same time.

YOU'RE THE TOP

Words and Music by Cole Porter

1st Chorus:

You're the top!
You're the Colosseum.
You're the top!
You're the Louvre Museum.

You're a melody
From a symphony by Strauss,
You're a Bendel bonnet,
A Shakespeare sonnet,
You're Mickey Mouse.

You're the Nile,
You're the Tow'r of Pisa,
You're the smile
On the Mona Lisa.

I'm a worthless check,
A total wreck, a flop,
But if, baby, I'm the bottom,
You're the top!

2nd Chorus:

You're the top!
You're Mahatma Gandhi;
You're the top!
You're Napoleon brandy,

You're the purple light
Of a summer night in Spain
You're the National Gall'ry,
You're Garbo's sal'ry,
You're cellophane.

You're sublime
You're a turkey dinner,
You're the time
Of the Derby winner.

I'm a toy balloon
That is fated soon to pop;
But if, baby, I'm the bottom,
You're the top!

CURRENT NEWS, TRENDS, AND MESSAGE SONGS

Songs that made use of timely topics and news headlines:

We Are the World (We Are the Children)
Still in Saigon
Blowin' in the Wind
Take This Job and Shove It

Trend songs:

Ghostbusters
Disco Duck
Itsy-Bitsy Teeny-Weeny, Yellow Polka-Dot Bikini

Songs that convey a message:

Born in the USA
What's Goin' On
We Are Family

PERSONAL EXPERIENCES

The following songs, trade rumor has it, are actual personal experiences of these famous writer-performers:

You're So Vain (Carly Simon)
Homeward Bound (Paul Simon)
By the Time I Get to Phoenix (Jim Webb)
At Seventeen (Janis Ian)

Writing from your own experience allows you to write about what you know best—*yourself*!

Sometimes it requires courage to share intimate feelings and confessions, but personal songs are probably the most honest and moving songs that can be written.

NOVELTY SONGS

A humorous combination of words and music can capture the country overnight. However, many of these songs are like meteors; they burn out quickly. For example:

Ob-La-Di, Ob-La-Da
Convoy
The Streak
Yellow Submarine
Tequila, Sheila

If there is a funny streak in your personality and you can express humor in a song, you have the opportunity to gain *instant* attention as a songwriter.

NAME SONGS

Whether the name of a song is *My Sharona, Ramona, Mandy, Candy, Michelle,* or *Bill,* people identify with name songs even though the name being used is not their name.

The subject matter in a name song permits the listener to pretend he or she is, or could be, the character in the song. The person relates to the characteristics of the personality rather than to the actual name.

CHARACTER SONGS

Songs about unusual people are always a challenge for songwriters. More important, they provoke interest and curiosity in the minds of the record-buying audience. Having an eccentric person, real or imagined, enter your life is an experience.

The following characters have stepped out of the imaginations of songwriters and left an indelible mark on the world of music (the only character from real life is *Vincent,* whose song is a tribute to Vincent Van Gogh, the renowned Dutch painter):

Delta Dawn
Mister Bojangles
Bad, Bad Leroy Brown
Mack the Knife
Eleanor Rigby
Vincent

Sooner or later, in our lifetime, most of us will meet or invent an imaginary offbeat character who is worthy of Tin Pan Alley immortality in song.

The following lyric was inspired by one such eccentric person. The theme of the lyric is *reincarnation*:

THE NEXT LIFE OF OTIS McRAY

Lyric by Buddy Kaye

Verse:

He was the old man who lived down the street
I'd see him most ev'ry day
His movements were slow and how little he'd eat
His frail body could almost blow away.
He had the wisdom and I had the time
And his words had the ring of a childhood rhyme.

Chorus: If one day you don't see me here
I'll be out there in the atmosphere
Over rooftops and tennis courts
So look for me in the weather reports
Just floating over city and town
And when it's time I'll touch on down
Back to this earth in another way
Here in the next life of Otis McRay.

2nd Chorus: You'll be much older next time we meet
On a train or a bus or just on the street
I may be taller and not so thin
A different man in a different skin
Hope you'll treat me the same nice way
Here in the next life of Otis McRay.

Extension: So don't look so sad now that I'm going away
I'll be back in the next life of Otis McRay.

STORY SONGS

As a songwriter your role as a storyteller is as important as that of any playwright, novelist, screenwriter, or newspaper reporter.

The story song differs from the character song because it has a larger framework than the one-person narrative. Harry Chapin, C. W. McCall, Bob Dylan, Pete Seeger, Woody Guthrie and Arlo Guthrie are some of the colorful writer-performers who have built their careers around story songs.

Inspiration for story songs can originate from newspaper stories, comic books, and magazine articles, as well as from your own experience.

Among the most famous recordings in this category are:

Lucille (Kenny Rogers)
The Gambler (Kenny Rogers)
Taxi (Harry Chapin)
Ode to Billy Joe (Bobbie Gentry)
Hotel California (The Eagles)
Alice's Restaurant (Arlo Guthrie)

Inspiration for a story song can also come from fiction. If you read Bret Harte's book of short stories, *The Luck of Roaring Camp,* you might be moved by his colorful descriptions of the Old West in the California Gold Rush days. Harte had a marvelous way of portraying a variety of people—miners, gamblers, bartenders, and prostitutes.

When you review the following lyric (based on Harte's stories), allow your mind to wander into the atmosphere of an old mining town.

PANNING FOR GOLD

Lyric by Buddy Kaye

Chorus: They came panning for gold . . . panning for gold
They talk it and they dream it,
But mostly they get old.
If the summer heat don't get 'em
Just wait till it gets cold.
You better be born lucky
When you're panning for gold.

Verse 1: That night at the Yellowrock Dance Hall
I'll tell it the way I heard it told
The miners were drinkin' and gamblin'
And playin' it loose, with chunks o' gold.

On the stand sat a guy honky-tonkin'
A fiddle and banjo played along.
The ladies were shriekin' and laughin'

And havin' a ball, while some painted doll
Was singin' a bawdy song.

(Repeat chorus.)

Verse 2: The work gang of Whiskey Hill Gold Mine
Jus' came bustin' in to join the fun
Well, there were just so many ladies
It turned out to be, two men for one.

One guy cut in on Big Yank and Dolly
That freak put his head right in a noose
'Cuz Yank was a heavyweight fighter
And when he let go, a hammerin' blow
In seconds all hell broke loose.

The Whiskey Hill Gang came out swingin'
The Yellowrock Miners took 'em on
The chairs and the tables went flyin'
And everything standing was gone.

(Repeat chorus.)

Verse 3: Then some preacher man screamed, "Gold is evil
And sinners are doomed to burn in Hell."
He may or may not, have reached the whole lot
But something had changed, you could tell.

Big Yank put his arms around Dolly
A reverence filled the crowded hall
That preacher man got them to thinkin'
That money and gold, just isn't all.

They went to their shacks in the mountains
The long days and the months and the years
Sometimes the younger ones cried, and the older ones died,
And the others just lived with their fears.

(Repeat chorus.)

MOTION PICTURE TITLES

The copyright law clearly states that titles cannot be copyrighted. There is nothing to prevent a songwriter from using a movie title for the creation of a song. It is not necessary for you to obtain permission from the motion picture company in order to do so.

However, it would not be advantageous to write a song using a film title if a title song already exists in the motion picture. It's a good idea to check carefully before starting to write the song.

Two classic situations have occurred:

One situation took place regarding the MGM film *Gone with the Wind*. Here is a lovely title. Yet, for some reason, the film producers never requested a title song. The theme song of the film was called *Tara's Theme*. ("Tara" was the name of the Southern plantation in the movie.) Two songwriters took advantage of this and wrote an outstanding song entitled *Gone with the Wind*. It has since become a standard.

A similar situation occurred with the title *The Treasure of Sierra Madre*. Warner Brothers (who released the film) liked the song that borrowed the title from the motion picture well enough to use it to promote the movie, even though the song itself was not in the film.

SPECIAL SITUATION SONGS

There will always be a vast market for special situation songs. New fads and events are always springing up.

Special situation songs include:

Happy Birthday to You
White Christmas

School Days
Easter Parade
Santa Claus Is Coming to Town
Take Me Out to the Ball Game
Surfin' USA

In addition, there are thousands of places you can glamorize in song. Hopefully your efforts will add to the following list of places already immortalized:

I Left My Heart in San Francisco
Moonlight in Vermont
California, Here I Come
Rocky Mountain High
St. Louis Blues
Chattanooga Choo-Choo
Galveston
Hooray for Hollywood
Shuffle off to Buffalo
Kansas City
Woodstock

ADDENDUM #2

Writing Assignments

ASSIGNMENT #1: ONE-SYLLABLE WORDS

The following assignment was designed to help you develop skill with words. Read the following carefully:

> When you come right down to it—there is no law that says you have to use big words when you write or talk. There are lots of small words, and good ones, that can be made to say all the things you want to say quite as well as the big ones. It may take a bit more time to find them at first but it can be well worth it—and we all know what they mean.

Stop for a minute. Reread it. Analyze it. What one thing strikes you as being unique and unusual about this paragraph? What do these words have in common?

You may have discovered that all the words in the above paragraph contain just *one* syllable.

Your assignment now is to present a strong case for words with one syllable. Describe what these short words can do for a lyric. Use only one-syllable words to make your point before you read the illustration of this unusual exercise invented by Joseph A. Ecclesine.

Small words can be crisp, brief, terse—go to the point, like a knife. They have a charm all their own. They dance, twist, turn, sing. Like sparks in the night, they light the way for the eyes of those who read. They are the grace notes of prose. Some make you feel, as well as see, the cold deep dark of night, the hot salt sting of tears. Small words move with ease, where big words stand still—or worse, bog down and get in the way of what you want to say. There is not much, in all truth, that small words will not say, and say quite well.

ADDITIONAL ASSIGNMENT FOR ONE-SYLLABLE WORDS

If you are convinced that one-syllable words can produce powerfully effective sentences, develop a lyric using the form of A–A–B–A (stanza, stanza, "bridge," stanza) using all one-syllable words.

Example: In the beautiful classic love song *My Heart Stood Still,* Richard Rodgers and Lorenz Hart innovatively, warmly used the one-syllable approach until the "bridge":

I took one look at you,
That's all I meant to do;
And then my heart stood still!

My feet could step and walk,
My lips could move and talk,
And yet, my heart stood still!

ASSIGNMENT #2: COLLECTING SONG TITLES

Your assignment is to become a "Song Title Collector," from now on. (Review *Technique #1*.)

Put your "antennae" to work. Each day, as you discover a title or two that appeals to you, transfer these titles to your master list of titles.

As you now know, titles are the songwriter's inventory. Your continually expanding title collection will serve as a constant reservoir of ideas and inspiration.

ASSIGNMENT #3: WRITING WORDS TO A HIT MELODY

If you don't plan to write music to your own words, consider writing lyrics to a popular hit melody on the charts. Substitute *your* words for the words in the song. Make sure you follow the same form, meter, rhyme scheme, and accents as in the original song.

This will introduce you to forms created by other writers. Eventually you can create your own lyrical structures and rhyme schemes.

This will also teach you how to complete a song without having a music collaborator at your side.

ASSIGNMENT #4: THE CHARACTER SONG

Using songs like *Mr. Bojangles* or *Delta Dawn* for inspiration, write a complete song or just a lyric about a person you know well.

The person or character in your lyric could be a family member, a friend, a fictionalized individual about whom you have read—perhaps someone who lives in your fantasy. Examples:

Someday My Prince Will Come
Angie Baby
Eleanor Rigby
Mack the Knife

An original story with crafted lyric lines has proven to have the power to hypnotize listeners as it weaves its narrative.

The Gambler, immortalized by Kenny Rogers, is an excellent example of a song that:

1. Touches many levels of consciousness.
2. Tells an interesting story.
3. Reveals character study.
4. Connects generations (the old storyteller and the young fellow-passenger).
5. Presents a lesson in the art of gambling—and in the "game" of life.

The record-buying public is fascinated by character songs which introduce them to people they would never have the opportunity to meet in real life.

ASSIGNMENT #5: THE COUNTRY SONG

Beginning with an imaginative title—a title that tells a story in itself, such as *Living Here, Loving There and Lying in Between*—create a country song that you consider to be "a slice of life" with a melody, a down-to-earth situation told in everyday language.

If you are writing a personal love song (omitting honky-tonk bars, no-tell motels, trucking, and other subjects indigenous to country songs), your song may have *crossover* potential. It may cross over to the Top 40 pop audience, to soul and even rock charts. (Review the special section on country music.)

Choose an artist for whom to write—one, preferably, with whom you can identify. Keep that artist in mind throughout the process of creating your song. If the song is a ballad, strive for emotional lines in your lyric. If you're writing a novelty song, be as original and as outrageous as you can.

If writing country songs is a new experience for you, saturate your mind by listening to local country music stations before you begin writing your own song in this category.

ASSIGNMENT #6: STAFF WRITING

When you have mastered the craft of songwriting and are professional enough to be hired by a music publisher as a staff writer, be prepared to accept writing assignments that you may not like, feel, or identify with.

Assignments can range from the title song for a movie, a play, an CD album, to perhaps a published book. Professional staff writers always find a way to meet the challenge and complete the assignment.

In a mock staff-writing assignment to a class at UCLA Extension, one song title was given to sixty students: *We Walked in Together (And I Walked Out Alone)*. The purpose was to prove that a title—any title—has an inexhaustible range of approaches that can be used as subject matter.

Sixty different lyrics were turned in for review. The subjects ranged from two miners in a mine explosion, Siamese twins being prepared for separation, the motion picture "Love Story" theme of Ryan O'Neal bringing Ali McGraw to the hospital, to a man walking into a psychiatrist's office with an inflated ego. The comical lyric that follows, reprinted by permission, was written by Dick Patterson, a gifted actor and brilliant satirist.

WE WALKED IN TOGETHER (AND I WALKED OUT ALONE)

Lyric by Dick Patterson

1st Verse:

Now it's a fact
I wasn't a real great act
Played guitar and sang in "C"
Through bad reviews
I got the news
My guitar was "carrying" me

Couldn't get a bookin'
Nothin' was cookin'
Our partnership was a flop
So I made the arrangement
For our last engagement
To play the Great Broadway—Pawn Shop

Chorus:

We walked in together
A day I could not postpone

Now the Hockshop Czar
Had my guitar
And I walked out alone.

We walked in together
My heart had turned to stone
The deal was quick
Even took my pick
And I walked out alone

2nd Verse: Between the I.O.U.'s
And the Payment Dues
I was swimmin' in a pool of mud
Sold my car
Then I went too far
And started selling my blood!

I began to weaken
My guitar started creakin'
Our duet had come to a stop . . .
Tired of the respite
I got desperate
And found the Great Broadway—Pawn Shop!

Chorus: We walked in together
And I walked out alone
Now the Old Money Lender
Has my Fender
And now I'm on my own.

We walked in together
And I walked out alone
Got forty bucks
Now, no more plucks
Yes, I'm on my own

Last Verse: Now every time
I pass that shop
I look the other way
But I'd hock my thumb

For one more strum
As I recall that day . . . when

We walked in together
What more can I say?
Now I'm the fella
Who sings a cappella
And my guitar's playing Broadway!

Dick Patterson's free-form lyric, though brilliant, is not considered commercial. Dick obviously approached it as a "fun" assignment. He succeeded admirably—a hearty laugh was had by all.

In synopsis form, choose an approach that appeals to you before you start writing your lyric for *We Walked in Together (And I Walked Out Alone).*

ASSIGNMENT #7: THE PERSONAL SONG

This assignment gives you the opportunity to write from your heart—what you feel, what you think, what is currently on your mind. Because it is personal, the song should be among the most pleasant experiences you enjoy as a songwriter, and also the easiest to write. (Review *Technique #18—Person-to-Person Lyrics.*)

Express a complaint in a love song, as in *You Don't Bring Me Flowers.* Open your heart, as in *I Love You More Today Than Yesterday.* Corral someone's attention who hasn't been listening to you, as in *You Turn Me Off Like a Radio.*

In writing personal songs, be careful not to confuse them with "private" songs that are personal only to you.

Think universally.

Personal songs are only universal if they touch a wide

range of feelings, emotions, and experiences common to most people. Universality is usually achieved when you write the truth about what you feel, what you know, where you have been, where you want to be, and what you have seen—the total experience of who you are.

ASSIGNMENT #8: THE NOVELTY SONG

The hit ingredient of a novelty song is luck. This is the main reason music publishers shy away from novelty songs.

On the other hand, having a hit novelty song is one of the quickest ways to gain national attention as a songwriter. Examples: Ray Stevens's *When You're Hot, You're Hot* and Roger Miller's *King of the Road.*

If your novelty song deals with a current event, it must be written within days of the incident, and recorded and played on the air in "record"-breaking time.

This may necessitate moving quickly into the business side of music as writer, artist, producer, record manufacturer, and sales "force" that delivers the finished product to record distributors and radio stations.

Your assignment is to choose a current event that is featured in today's newspaper headlines. Serious as that may be, make your lyrical point of view comical, satirical, or tongue-in-cheek.

EXAMPLE: when the gasoline shortage became an irritant to the public some years ago, Jerry Reed wrote *Who Is the Man Who Put the Line in Gasoline?* Ray Stevens came up with *The Streak* when those shenanigans became a craze.

ASSIGNMENT #9: NAME SONG

Write a name song about someone you know, or would like to know. It can be a love song, a character song, a fun song.

When it has been polished to your satisfaction, present it to that person. Request his or her reaction.

You will soon find out from that person's comments whether or not you have captured his or her personality, idiosyncrasies, and so forth. And if there is a message in your song, you will learn if you were on target.

ASSIGNMENT #10: STORY SONG

Scan your local newspaper. Read short stories. Delve into magazines. Select a theme for a story song.

Draw a synopsis from the story you wish to write, select a form, and make every line count.

It should inspire you to learn that the hit song *Tie a Yellow Ribbon 'Round the Old Oak Tree* made its first public appearance as a true story in *Reader's Digest*.

ASSIGNMENT #11: SPECIAL SITUATION SONG

You are surrounded with special situations. The things you observe may have unlimited possibilities.

Write about your town or city if it is special to you. Write about nature, compassion for all living things. Write about sports. There has never been a popular song about the exhilaration of mountain skiing or the games soccer and hockey, or the fun of ice skating. (Review the section on special situation songs in *Addendum #1—What to Write About.*)

ASSIGNMENT #12: WRITING A SONG FROM A TV SHOW

Your assignment is to extract a dramatic scene or intimate sequence from a television movie.

Soap operas, presented daily, are filled with potential song titles and real-life dramas.

Draw an idea, title, or situation from one of these shows. Build your information into the kind of song that you believe will have universal appeal.

Use every technique to enhance your lyric.

When your lyric is completed to your satisfaction, add suitable music.

> If you want to sell
>   what John Doe buys
> You must see the world
>   through John Doe's eyes

Epilogue

Writing the Song

If you have been faithful in following the guidelines of *Method Songwriting,* you should now be prepared to exercise the fundamental mechanics of good songwriting.

Answers should come to mind almost immediately when dealing with questions about your songs:

- Do I have a unique title? A fresh story approach?
- Shall I begin with a verse or "hook" chorus?
- Do I have all the details for my verses?
- Where shall I place my title to make it memorable?
- Do I have a melodic idea for an explosive "hook" chorus?

When you have mastered the mechanics and strategies of *Method Songwriting,* all your energies will be applied to the development of your ideas. Compare it to the experienced woodcarver, who concentrates on his design rather than concerning himself with the slipping of the blade.

Method Songwriting's techniques were created so that they can always be applied to the current trend, style, and language of the contemporary market. Constantly listening to music that is current will make you aware of what is commercially acceptable.

Whether you write songs for the pure joy of it, or you dream of commercial acceptance and financial success, your finished product should be a statement of professional literacy to make you competitive in the market, as well as personally proud of your accomplishments.

Song-Correcting Guide—To Help You Write a Hit Song

A. Use this worksheet as your "self-correcting" system.

B. Constantly review the twenty techniques as they apply to your song.

TECHNIQUES:

#1 STARTING WITH A TITLE	Are you proud of your title? Is it unusual? Original? Provocative? Does it have universal appeal?
#2 WORKING FROM A SYNOPSIS	Are you comfortable with your story? Have you tried other approaches or new storylines using the same title?
#3 THREE-MINUTE MOVIE	Have you established a solid *Beginning*: (problem or conflict), *Middle*: (effects of the problem), and *End*: (solution, resolution)?
#4 ASSOCIATED WORDS	Have you listed words and phrases that connect with the *key* word in your title? Research *Roget's Thesaurus* for more.
#5 FORM/STRUCTURE	Have you experimented with various *forms* to establish the most effective one for your title and lyric to follow?
#6 TITLE REPETITION	Remember! In form A–B–A–B it is best to use your title in the first line of your "hook" chorus. In form A–A–B–A use your song title in line 1 or line 4 and in repeated "A" stanzas.

#7
METER and SYLLABLES

Meter: Check rhythm pattern for accented and *un*accented words in your first verse or stanza to be certain that they correspond with verses or stanzas that follow.

Syllables: Count the syllables in first verse or stanza to avoid errors matching up your lyrics to repeated sections.

#8
RHYMES

The rule is: Once used, a rhyme should not be used again in another section. Always use the rhyme that will provide the strongest line of thought and reason.

#9
SINGABLE WORDS

Sing your lyrics aloud at an accelerated pace. Check for words that do not flow gracefully.

#10
SPECIFICS

Check information you want to cover in your lyric:
Who?________________________
What?_______________________
When?_______________________
Where?______________________
Why?________________________
How?________________________

#11
IMAGERY

Scrutinize lines that may be changed for more picturesque words or phrases. Work with *Roget's Thesaurus* or a phrase finder.

#12
ALLITERATION

Words produce a pleasant sounding effect when they begin with the same letter. Work with a thesaurus or synonym finder to substitute one word for another.

#13
LANGUAGE TONE

Review your choice of words and colloquial expressions for precise regional conversation.

#14
EMOTIONAL VALUES

If the aim of your lyric is to "move" your listener, it must first "move" you. Check your lyric for truth, honesty, sensitivity, originality.

#15
OPENING LINES THAT COMMAND ATTENTION

Does the first line of your lyric have impact? Is it amusing? Thought-provoking? Have you made an interesting statement to pique the curiosity of the passive listener?

#16
OVERSTATING

List your "larger-than-life" statements and you'll be heard.

#17
BREVITY

Are your lines economically stated? Do your lines:
(A) Express a complete thought and (B) Advance the story?

#18
PERSON-TO-PERSON LYRICS

Have you directed your lyric to one person? The emotional power of intimate expressions makes it almost mandatory that you experiment with rewriting your second- or third-person lyrics.

#19
CHANGING LYRICAL SCENES

Have you brought your lyric stanzas or verses into another time? Found another location? Introduced another person? Another idea?

#20
PROSODY

Does your music catch the spirit of the mood and intention of your lyric?

The Songwriter's Glossary

ADMINISTRATION: The management of all financial, copyright, and contractual aspects of either an entire catalog or a particular song.

ADVANCE: Money paid prior to the release or recording of a song, to be deducted against future royalties of that song.

AF OF M: American Federation of Musicians; union for arrangers, contractors, copyists, musicians, and orchestrators.

AFTRA: American Federation of Television and Radio Artists; union for actors, announcers, narrators, singers, and sound effects artists.

ANGEL: The financial backer of a play.

ARRANGEMENT: A new version of a composition for performance by other instruments and voices.

ARTIST: Individual or group under recording contract.

ASCAP: American Society of Composers, Authors and Publishers; a performing rights organization that collects royalties from users for writers and publishers.

ASSIGNMENT: The transfer of rights to a song or catalog from one copyright proprietor to another.

BILLBOARD: A music industry trade publication.

BLACK: Music traditionally performed by black artists; also called rhythm and blues or soul music.

BMI: Broadcast Music, Inc.; a performing rights organization that collects royalties from users for writers and publishers.

BOOKING AGENT: One who seeks employment for artists from buyers of talent.

BOOTLEGGING: The unauthorized recording and selling of a performance of a song.

BRIDGE: A connecting passage between two sections of a composition.

BULLET: Designation of a record listed on the charts, referring to increased record sales.

CASSETTE: A small case containing magnetic tape for recording.

CATALOG: All songs owned by a music publisher considered as one collection.

CD: Compact disc.

CHARTS: Lists published in trade magazines of the best-selling records. There are separate charts for classical, country and western, inspirational, jazz, pop, and soul.

CHORD: A combination of three or more notes sounded together in harmony.

CHORUS: A section of a song repeated at certain intervals.

CLEARANCE: The right of a radio station to play a song.

CLICK TRACK: A perforated soundtrack that produces click sounds that enable one to hear a predetermined beat in synchronization with a movie.

CMA: Country Music Association; organization devoted to promoting country music.

COLLABORATOR: One of two or more partners in song composition.

COMMERCIAL: Strong sales potential; that which has mass appeal.

COMPOSER: Writer of music.

COMPOSITION: A work of music; the art of writing music.

COMPULSORY LICENSE (PHONORECORDS): Statutory mandate given to a copyright owner to permit third parties to make sound recordings of the copyright owner's song after it has been recorded once.

COPYRIGHT: The exclusive rights granted to authors and composers for protection of their works; to secure protection for a composition by filing the proper registration forms with the Copyright Office.

COPYRIGHT INFRINGEMENT: The unauthorized use of another's copyrighted material.

COPYRIGHT NOTICE: Notice comprised of three elements:

(1) the symbol of copyright (©), the word "copyright," or the abbreviation "Corp.";
(2) the year the song has been registered for copyright or the year of first publication of the work; and
(3) the copyright owner's name.

COPYRIGHT OFFICE: Department of federal government whose primary responsibility is to file and supply information regarding copyrights.

COPYRIGHT OWNER: The owner of any one of the exclusive rights comprised in a copyright.

COPYRIGHT ROYALTY TRIBUNAL: A committee created by Public Law 94-553 to determine adjustments starting January 1, 1978, of royalty rates with respect to compulsory licenses for educational television, cable television jukeboxes, and sound recordings.

COVER RECORD: Another artist's version of a previously recorded song.

CROSSOVER: A song receiving airplay in more than one regional area.

CUT: To record; a specific recording selection.

C & W: Country and western music.

DAT: Digital Audio Tape

DEMO: A demonstration recording used to show a song's potential to music industry personnel.

DISTRIBUTOR: Company that exclusively handles the sale of a record company's product to jobbers and retail outlets for a certain territory.

EMPLOYEE-FOR-HIRE: Contractural agreement whereby a motion picture producer or company employs a composer or lyricist to create music or songs for a movie with copyright ownership to be retained by the producer or company.

ENGINEER: Individual who operates studio equipment during the recording of a song.

FOLIO: A collection of printed songs offered for sale to the public.

FORMAT: Professional term applied to the type of music played primarily on a radio station: rock and roll, country, black, classical, jazz, pop, etc.

GOLD ALBUM: Certification by the Recording Industry Association of America that an album has sold a half million units.

GOLD SINGLE: Certification by the Recording Industry Association of America that a single has sold one half million units.

GRAMMY: Music industry awards presented annually by the National Academy of Recording Arts and Sciences (NARAS).

GROOVE: Rhythm, beat, or tempo creating the "feel" of the song.

HARMONY: The combination of musical notes to form chords that enhance the melodic line.

HARRY FOX AGENCY: An organization that represents music publishers in connection with the mechanical reproduction of their copyrights as well as the use of their compositions for motion-picture synchronication.

"HEAD" ARRANGEMENT: A spontaneously created arrangement without instrumental and vocal charts. Instead, the musicians read the lead sheets and an arrangement is made from various stylings devised in the studio.

HOOK: A phrase or melody line repeating itself in a song; the "catchy" part to a song.

JINGLE: A brief musical phrase usually accompanied by lyrics used to convey a commercial message.

KEY: A system of related notes based on and named after a note forming a scale; the main tonality of a song.

LABEL: Another name for a record company. "What label does she record for?"

LASS: Los Angeles Songwriters Showcase; a nonprofit organization providing songwriters relevant information and opportunities to exhibit their works before music industry personnel.

LEADERED TAPE: Reel-to-reel tape containing songs separated by white tape for easy access.

LEAD SHEET: A musical notation of a song's melody along with the chord symbols, words, and other pertinent information.

LICENSE: A legal document granting permission to engage in an activity otherwise unlawful; to authorize by formal license.

LICK: A brief, improvised musical interpolation or flourish.
LOGO: A clipped form of logotype; a unique company signature or trademark found on records and tapes identifying the company issuing the product.
LP: A long-playing record played at 33⅓ revolutions per minute (rpm).
LYRICIST: A writer of lyrics, also called lyrist.
LYRICS: The words to a song.
LYRIC SHEET: A typed copy of song lyrics.

MANAGER: One who advises and guides an artist in developing his career.
MARKET: Selling place; medium where only one type of music is played (i.e., classical, country and western, jazz, pop, rhythm and blues, etc.)
MASTER: The finished version of a song, after mixing, from which records are pressed and distributed to record stores and radio stations.
MECHANICAL RIGHT: Right granted by U.S. copyright law to a copyright owner to profit from the mechanical reproduction of his song.
MECHANICAL RIGHTS ORGANIZATION: Collection agency for copyright owners of moneys earned from the mechanical (video, tape, disc, records, etc.) reproduction of their songs.
MECHANICAL ROYALTIES: Moneys earned for use of a copyright in mechanical reproductions, mostly records and tapes.
MIDI: Musical Instrument Digital Interface; electronic connection of instruments allowing one to be played by another.
MIX: To blend the tracks of a multitrack recording.
MODULATE: To change keys in a song.
MOR: Middle of the Road; songs classified as easy listening.
MOTIF: The shortest significant melody of a song or theme.
MOVIOLA: A small machine used for viewing and editing motion-picture film.
MTV: Music Television; a cable network broadcasting music videos and artist information.
MTW: Musical Theatre Works, Inc.; a nonprofit, New York–based organization dedicated to the development of original theater music.
MUSIC PUBLISHER: The individual or company who:

1. screens songs and gets them commercially recorded;
2. exploits the copyrights;
3. protects the copyrights; and
4. collects income from performance, mechanical, synchronization, and printing rights both in the United States and in foreign countries.

NARAS: National Academy of Recording Arts and Sciences; a professional organization that monitors popularity of released recordings.

NEUTRAL DEMO: A demonstration recording that doesn't sound as if it is for one particular artist, but represents the song whereby it can be recorded by anyone.

NEW AGE: Contemporary electronic or synthesized music for meditation and relaxation.

NSAI: Nashville Songwriters Association International; an organization that helps new and professional country songwriters.

ONE-STOP: Wholesale record dealer selling records of several manufacturers to jukebox operators and record stores.

ON SPEC: On speculation; unsolicited material voluntarily written without a contract.

OVERDUB: The addition of instruments or voices to pre-existing tracks.

PAYOLA: Secret payment to broadcasters to play certain records.

PERFORMANCE ROYALTIES: Moneys earned from use of one's songs on radio, television, and other users of music.

PERFORMING RIGHT: Right granted by U.S. copyright law which states that one may not publicly perform a copyrighted musical work without the owner's permission.

PERFORMING RIGHTS ORGANIZATION: British organization whose purpose is to collect moneys earned from public performances of songs by users of music and to distribute these to the writers and publishers of these songs in proportions accurately reflecting the amount of a song's performances, similar to ASCAP and BMI.

PHONORECORD: A sound transmission device other than that accompanying a motion picture or other audiovisual work.

PHOTO-OFFSET REPRODUCTION: Reproduction of musical manuscript by printing press.

PICK: A song projected to have success after being reviewed in the trades.

PIRATING: The unauthorized reproduction and selling of sound recording (i.e., records and tapes).

PITCH: To audition or sell; the position of a tone in the musical scale.

PLATINUM ALBUM: Certification by the Recording Industry Association of America that an album has sold one million units.

PLATINUM SINGLE: Certification by the Recording Industry Association of America that a single has sold two million units.

PLUG: A promotional advertisement; a push for a song's performance.

POINTS: A percentage of money producers and artists earn based on the retail list price of 90 percent of all records sold.

PRESS: The manufacture of a large quantity of records duplicated from a master for commercial sale.

PRODUCER: The individual who supervises the making of a record from selection of the song to its completion as a master.

PROFESSIONAL MANAGER: The person in charge of screening new material for music publishers and of obtaining commercial recording of songs in his company's catalog.

PROGRAM DIRECTOR: Radio station employee who determines which songs will be broadcast.
PUBLICATION: The printing and distribution of copies of a work to the public by sale, transfer of ownership, rental, lease, or lending.
PUBLIC DOMAIN: Material unprotected by copyright due to an expired copyright or caused by an invalid copyright notice.

RACK JOBBER: Dealer supplying records of many manufacturers to certain retail outlets such as drug stores, variety stores, and supermarkets.
RAP: Lyrics energetically delivered by a performer against a strong rhythm background.
RELEASE: The issuing of a record by a record company.
R & B: Rhythm and blues; soul music.
RHYMING DICTIONARY: A compilation of words arranged by like sound.
RIAA: Recording Industry Association of America; monitors sales and distributes gold and platinum records to performers, songwriters, and others involved in hit records.
RIFF: A constantly repeated musical phrase used as background for a soloist or as the basic theme of a final chorus.
ROYALTY: Money earned from use of a record or song.

SELF-CONTAINED ARTIST: An artist who writes and performs his own material.
SESAC: Society of American Songwriters and Composers, a performing rights, mechanical rights, and synchronization licensing organization.
SESSION: A meeting where musicians and vocalists make a recording.
SGA: Songwriters Guild of America, an organization providing contractual guidelines for songwriters, royalty collections, and copyright renewal services.
SHEET MUSIC: Printed copies of a single song offered for public sale.
SHOWCASE: A presentation of new songs and/or talent.
SINGLE: A small record played at 45 rpm containing two selections, one on each side; record released because of record company expectations that the "A" side would be successful.
SLEEPER: A song that unexpectedly becomes popular.
SONG PLUGGER: A professional music person, employed by a music publisher, who auditions songs for performers.
SONG SHARK: One who profits from dealing with songwriters by deceptive methods.
SPLIT PUBLISHING: When the publishing rights to a song are divided among two or more publishers.
STAFF WRITING: A salaried writer working exclusively for a publisher.
STANDARD: A song that continues to be popular for years.

STATUTORY COPYRIGHT: Status acquired by a composition when it is registered with the Copyright Office or is published with the proper copyright notice.
STUDIO: A place where music is recorded.
SUBPUBLISHING: When the original publisher contracts his song or catalog to be handled by a foreign publisher for that territory.
SWEETEN: To add new parts, such as strings and horns, to existing rhythm and vocal tracks.
SYNCHRONIZATION: The placing of music in timed relation to film.
SYNCHRONIZATION RIGHT: The right to use a musical composition in (timed relation to) a film or videotape.

TAKE: A recording attempt; an accepted recording of a musical or vocal section.
TOP 40: Radio station format where records played are only those contained in lists of the best-selling records.
TOP 100: Lists published in the trades of the top-selling singles for a particular market.
TRACK: One of the several components of recording tape that contains recorded sounds, which is mixed with the other tracks for a finished recording of the song; the recording of all the instruments or vocals of a particular musical section; music and/or voices previously recorded.
TRADES: Music industry publications.

UNION SCALE: Minimum wage scale earned in employment by members of AFTRA, AF of M, etc.

VCR: Video cassette recorder.
VH-1: Video Hits 1; a cable channel broadcasting contemporary music videos.

Acknowledgments continued from page iv.

"I Love You, Honey, Let's Go Home," words by Buddy Kaye, music by Archie Jordan, © 1988 Budd Music Corp. All rights reserved. Used by permission.

"I Will Survive," written by Dino Fekaris and Freddie Perren, © 1978, 1979 Bibo Music Publishers and Perren-Vibes Music, Inc. (c/o The Welk Music Group, Santa Monica, CA 90401). International copyright secured. All rights reserved. Used by permission.

"In Real Life," written by Kent Robbins, © 1984 Hall-Clement Publications (c/o The Welk Music Group, Santa Monica, CA 90401). International copyright secured. All rights reserved. Used by permission.

"Just Gettin' Started," words by Buddy Kaye, music by Chuck Sabatino, © 1988 Budd Music Corp. All rights reserved. Used by permission.

"Lyin' Eyes," words and music by Don Henley and Glenn Frey, © 1975 Cass County Music & Red Cloud Music. All rights reserved. Used by permission.

"My Funny Valentine," by Richard Rodgers & Lorenz Hart, © 1937 by Chappell & Co., Inc. Copyright renewed. International copyright secured. All rights reserved. Used by permission.

"My Heart Stood Still," words by Lorenz Hart, music by Richard Rodgers, © 1927 (Renewed) Warner Bros., Inc. All rights reserved. Used by permission.

"The Next Life of Otis McRay," words by Buddy Kaye, © 1988 Budd Music Corp. All rights reserved. Used by permission.

"The Old Songs," words and music by David Pomeranz and Buddy Kaye, © 1981 WB Music Corp./Upward Spiral Music/Budd Music Corp. All rights reserved. Used by permission.

"One for My Baby (And One More for the Road)," by Harold Arlen and Johnny Mercer, © 1943 Harwin Music, © Renewed 1971 Harwin Music Co. International copyright secured. All rights reserved. Used by permission.

"Over the Rainbow," composer E. Y. Harburg and H. Arlen, © 1938, 1939 (Renewed 1966, 1967) Metro-Goldwyn-Mayer, Inc. Assigned to SBK Catalogue Partnership. Rights throughout the World controlled and administered by SBK Feist Catalog. International copyright secured. Made in U.S.A. All rights reserved. Used by permission.

"Panning for Gold," words by Buddy Kaye, © 1988 Budd Music Corp. All rights reserved. Used by permission.

"The Perfect Woman," words and music by Buddy Kaye and Philip Springer, © 1988 Budd Music Corp./Tamir Music. All rights reserved. Used by permission.

"Rhinestone Cowboy," words and music by Larry Weiss, © 1973, 1974 WB Music Corp. & House of Weiss Music Co. All rights reserved. Used by permission.

"Sing," words and music by Joe Raposo, © 1971 by Jonico Music, Inc. Used by permission.

"Someone You Once Loved," words by Buddy Kaye, © 1988 Budd Music Corp. All rights reserved. Used by permission.

"Tangerine," words and music by Johnny Mercer and Victor Schertzinger, © 1942 by Famous Music Corporation; Copyright renewed 1969 by Famous Music Corporation. All rights reserved. Used by permission.

"Teach Me Tonight," words by Sammy Cahn, music by Gene DePaul, © 1954, renewed 1982 by Hub Music Company. All rights reserved. Used by permission.

"Tennessee Girls," by Buddy Kaye, © 1988 Budd Music Corp. All rights reserved. Used by permission.

"These Foolish Things (Remind Me of You)," words by Holt Marvell, music by Jack Strachey and Harry Link, © 1935 Bossey and Co. Ltd., London, England. Copyright renewed. All rights for United States, Canada and Newfoundland assigned to Bourne Co., New York, NY. All rights reserved. International copyright secured. Used by permission.

"Thoughtless," words by Buddy Kaye, © 1946 Budd Music Corp. All rights reserved. Used by permission.

"Three's a Crowd," by Harry Warren, Al Dubin and Irving Kahal, © 1931 (Renewed) Warner Bros. Inc. All rights reserved. Used by permission.

"The Uninvited Guest," words by Buddy Kaye, music by Jeff Tweel, © 1988 CBS Songs/Budd Music Corp. All rights reserved. Used by permission.

"We Walked In Together (And I Walked Out Alone)," words by Dick Patterson, © 1988 by Dick Patterson. All rights reserved. Used by permission.

"We're Off to See the Wizard," composer E. Y. Harburg and H. Arlen, © 1938, 1939 (Renewed 1966, 1967) Metro-Goldwyn-Mayer, Inc. Assigned to SBK Catalogue Partnership. Rights throughout the World controlled and administered by SBK Feist Catalog. International copyright secured. Made in U.S.A. All rights reserved. Used by permission.

"The Wind Beneath My Wings," words and music by Larry Henley and Jeff Silbar, © 1981, 1983 Warner House of Music & WB Gold Music Corp. All rights reserved. Used by permission.

"Windmills of Your Mind," composer M. Legrand, M. Bergman, A. Bergman, © 1968 United Artist Music Co., Inc. All rights assigned to SBK Catalogue Partnership. All rights controlled and administered by SBK U Catalog. International copyright secured. Made in U.S.A. All rights reserved. Used by permission.

"The Year of the Cat," by Al Stewart and Peter Wood, © 1976 by UniChappell Music Inc., and Dick James Music. International copyright secured. All rights reserved. Used by permission.

"You Must Have Been a Beautiful Baby," words by Johnny Mercer, music by Harry Warren, © 1938 (Renewed) Warner Bros. Inc. All rights reserved. Used by permission.

"You're Getting to Be a Habit With Me," words by Al Dubin, music by Harry Warren, © 1932 (Renewed) Warner Bros. Inc. All rights reserved. Used by permission.

"You're the Top," words and music by Cole Porter, © 1934 (Renewed) Warner Bros. Inc. All rights reserved. Used by permission.